Tami Gilbert

Career CPR:
Meaningful Strategies to
Resuscitate or Nurture Your Career

by
Tami Gilbert

Tami Gilbert

Inquiries should be addressed to:

Dream World Press
c/o Tami Gilbert
P.O. Box 106
Highland Park, IL 60035
Printed in the United States of America

ISBN-13: 978-0-9967765-1-6

Table of Contents

Introduction

When we start a new job, we feel excited, passionate, and motivated, but somewhere along the way, we sometimes lose that excitement before we give ourselves the chance to succeed. As a result, we begin to feel dissatisfied with our career.

Many factors might change our motivation and drive to achieve career success. For example, sometimes the work environment, people, and circumstances become intolerable and begin to take their toll. Our motivation wanes, and we might wonder if we will ever reach our desired career destination. We begin to doubt ourselves.

Many people struggle to find a job and career path that inspires them, makes them happy, and motivates them to succeed. (I know far too many people who are unhappy with their job.)

Many people:
- have difficulty finding another job
- feel stuck in a job they dislike
- take a job that is merely a *job*
- accept a job that pays the same or less than they earn now
- can't find work close to where they live

- might like their job but have no passion for it

Whether you are looking for your first job, switching careers, or re-entering the job market, the job search process is challenging. Remember that looking for employment is a full-time job. Therefore, you need to approach job seeking as if you were looking for your dream job. When you are energized, your job search process is more enjoyable and fruitful and you are more likely to find success, as potential employers will sense your enthusiasm, confidence, and commitment.

In today's corporate environment, the workplace is changing so employees oftentimes feel disengaged at work: They grow frustrated with uncertain circumstances, including lack of long-term job stability, and/or are expected to do more work for the same amount of or *less* money.

The employment outlook is dynamic and responds to current economic conditions in the United States and abroad. During periods of economic stability and growth, employers' confidence enables them to increase hiring. During times of economic turmoil, mass layoffs, downsizing, and a lack of new hiring might slow down the job market. However, even during an economic decline, most employers will look out for quality talent.

Since we spend one third of our lives working, it is important for us to be happy with what we do. To write this book, I conducted extensive research, as well as incorporated ideas from my three decades of work experience, to give you several strategies that can help you fall in love with your current job or assist you in finding another one. My strategies to resuscitate and nurture your career *and* improve your happiness at work, at home, and in life include how to:

- Prepare for a company merger, layoff, turnover, promotion, etc.
- Work with difficult people, e.g., your supervisor or colleague
- Handle tough work situations
- Become an asset in your organization
- Be marketable in today's corporate America

According to "Four Keys to Happiness in Your Job" by Odesk CEO and thought leader Gary Swart, the four keys to job happiness are:

- Impact
- Growth and Development

- Financial Reward
- Work-Life Balance

The importance of weighing each area varies by individual and changes over a person's career, so assess yourself at each interval and on a regular basis. These four keys to happiness in our jobs may explain why only a few employees are engaged at work. An assumption is most employees' needs for professional and personal development are not met.

Having been in the professional world for 30+ years, I have learned that in the business environment, there's no room for slacking off. There's always someone who might do your job better, be more efficient, and have a more strategic technique for executing an important task.

Merely *thinking* about how involved you have to be to reach your desired career destination can be exhausting. Whether you are employed or unemployed, managing your career is a full-time responsibility.

Fortunately, you can learn how to feel more rewarded and fulfilled in your career, as you can use valuable strategies to breathe new life into a job you dislike.

We must reevaluate our jobs or careers. One way to do that is to answer one important question: Is your job on life support, i.e., are you just going through the motions with your job or career? From the job search to the job offer, this book provides tips to help you develop a strategic job search process and/or resuscitate your career.

Think about your career and where you want to be in 5, 10, 15, or 20 years. What is required of you to get there? More skills, more education, more experience? If you see yourself working in the same profession and enjoying it, you're where you need to be. Remaining in the same career does not mean staying in the same position. Aim high, and watch your career and happiness flourish. Life is too short for us to suffer every day in a job we dislike.

I believe that sustaining a successful career requires constant nurturing. We all desire and deserve to live our life to the fullest, and part of the equation involves maintaining and sustaining high performance at work so we can realize our potential.

Career management is a journey, but only those equipped to tackle the journey will persevere and reach their career goals, dreams, and aspirations!

Chapter 1
Symptoms and Side Effects

Heartburn

According to the Bureau of Labor Statistics, the average person spends one-third of his or her life at work. And many American workers spend, on average, more than 8.9 hours working or in work-related activities, 2 to 3 hours commuting to and from work, 7.7 hours sleeping 2.5 hours doing leisure / sports activities, and 1.2 hours caring for family and others. Consequently, the average person spends much more time at *work* than either sleeping or doing other things in their lives.

Furthermore, a 2013 Gallup poll found that, among American workers, only 30% considered themselves "engaged" at work, while 70% considered themselves disengaged and not reaching full potential there. These are sobering statistics in a still-struggling economy.

And an uncertain economy and company layoffs have put many workers in an unexpected predicament – and economic conditions, need, or other life events can cause them to choose a career path for which they have no passion. Therefore, they may become negative when they feel stuck in a dead-end job, earn less than they expect, or simply feel unappreciated. This employment uncertainty suddenly forces workers to re-evaluate their careers.

According to a Deloitte's Shift Index survey, most people are dissatisfied with their jobs, but only a few people have the courage to change careers: They just grin and bear their circumstances. Although these statistics may appear dreary, there is always hope.

Choose a job you love or can learn to love. Whether you are in a job you dislike, pursuing a promotion or a raise, or facing the middle of a job search, taking action can help you become a happier employee or even a dynamic entrepreneur.

Burnout

When I began my nursing career, people at work were like family to me. My coworkers and I were so close, we would go to each other's personal events, like weddings, funerals, children's graduations, and personal celebrations. The workplace was a place where I could get support from my colleagues.

However, today's workplace has changed dramatically: It is stricter and more business-like. Many people seem tense, on guard, and preoccupied with their own issues.

Job burnout can result from various factors, including lack of control and inability to influence decisions that affect one's job: work schedule, work assignments, or workload, lack of resources to do the work, and/or unclear job expectations. If you are uncertain about the degree of authority you have or what your supervisor or others expect from you, you are likely to feel uncomfortable at work, which can cause you stress. And we tend to experience burnout because modern technology makes it difficult for us to turn off our connections to our jobs, our friends, and the world. We work more now, so even while on vacation, we are on our laptops and mobile phones, never disconnecting from our jobs.

The result of these modern workplace changes leads to job burnout. The increasingly hostile and demanding environments in which we work are usually the cause of burnout. You may be experiencing job burnout if you answer "yes" to any of the following questions:

- Are you bored with your job?
- Does your job often keep you up at night?

- Have your sleep habits or appetite changed?
- When thinking about your job, do you feel bad about yourself?
- How do you feel when it is time to go to work? Do you become mentally or physically sick when thinking about work?
- Do you work in a dysfunctional office environment?
- Do you miss work or call in sick frequently?
- Do you experience the following symptoms?
  - Muscle tension
  - Anxiety or irritability
  - Stomach problems
  - Trouble concentrating

I remember working in a toxic environment. The workload was horrific, we had no say-so in the decision-making and went unappreciated, and there was a perceived lack of fairness. In addition, there was no empathy for the frontline workers or staff from the management for the work that needed to be done. And there was great tension among the employees because only a few employees were actually getting their work done while others were getting away with not carrying their load. This toxic work environment resulted from poor management, and the employees turned against each other. Workers were left to fend for themselves, so many employees were burned out.

Workers in some professions experience job burnout more than others. From my experience, human services professionals with high levels of burnout include surgeons, social workers, nurses, teachers, lawyers, engineers, physicians, customer service representatives, and police officers. One main reason that burnout is so prevalent within the human services field is because of the high-stress work environment and emotional demands of the job. Occupational burnout often develops slowly and is not recognized until it has become severe.

If you think you are experiencing job burnout, do not ignore your symptoms. Consult your doctor or a mental health provider. Many of us are overworked and burned out at our jobs because we do not know when or how to tell someone "no." During your career, there will be unreasonable requests, so you must know when to decline them tactfully and respectfully. (This does not mean you cannot accept the opportunity in the future.) Focus on making your career more exciting, but also avoid burnout.

Chapter 2
Attitude Temperature

According to Monster.com's senior writer John Rossheim, what is missing for many American workers today is passion – a positive emotional connection to their work. Passion comes from within you and includes your enthusiasm, drive, and motivation. If you feel passionate about your job, you apply your energy, skills, and drive to lead you toward success. Your success comes not so much from what you do (your job) but how well you do it and how passionate you are about it. And your passion attracts positive people who can help you advance your career.

One of my favorite quotes, "When you do what you love, you will never work a day in your life" (author unknown), indicates that you have a better chance of enjoying your career when you work in a profession you like. Therefore, take some time to ask yourself these questions:

- What have I always wanted to do?
- What is my work passion?
- Is my job a position, merely a way to pay the bills, or a stepping stone to a better career?

You feel empowered and energized about your career if you answer "yes" to the following questions:

- Are you fired up and ready to get back to work?
- Do you often feel motivated to work late to ensure you complete your work on time?
- Does the day seem to fly by because you are engaged in your work?
- Do you look forward to seeing your coworkers or working independently?

These are characteristics of people who love what they do and are not in their job only for the money.

> "Find what you like to do in your career and do the best job possible and seek work environments that are positive and growth promoting."
> — Megan M. Krischke, Contributor and Writer for *AMN Healthcare, Inc.* Magazine

Loving your career feels wonderful. This includes feeling fulfilled at work and liked, as well as comfortable with your colleagues, your supervisor, and the company. Job satisfaction is very important, so I advise clients to pursue a career they are passionate about.

Career Checkup: Performing a Few Tests

You might have a depressed career if you feel bad or depressed when you think about your job. Be aware of early warning signs that may slow down your work performance, and ask yourself these questions:

- Am I thorough and detail-oriented?
- Have I lost my desire to compete or stay competitive in the workplace?
- Do I wake up each morning, wishing my work were more satisfying? (When work is satisfying, it automatically feels natural and makes you feel successful. Remember, though, that satisfying work may not always be easy work.)
- Do I want a career that means more to me than a paycheck?
- Do I long for more appreciation, recognition, and rewards at work?
- Do I want true career bliss?

Warning Signs
Complacency

Dictionary.com defines complacency as "a feeling of quiet pleasure or security, often while unaware of some potential danger, defect, or the like; self-satisfaction or smug satisfaction with an existing situation, condition, etc." Complacency is the way of just going through the motions of going to work day in and day out and not investing in yourself professionally or improving your skills to get better at your job – the danger being you can derail your career. You might be losing motivation to compete in an ever-changing corporate world. If you aren't careful, you can easily fall into career or job complacency. Overcoming complacency boils down to two things: Staying determined and becoming ambitious. The second you lose either one, you have, essentially, given up on your career.

Are you in danger of sabotaging your career because you are complacent? If you are dissatisfied with your job, try to identify the root causes and career saboteurs. For example, perhaps you have:
- Become disengaged and disgruntled
- Discontinued your professional investment
- Avoided taking risks
- Lost hope
- Felt no passion for the work
- Started taking shortcuts (this may be a sign you may have a depressed career)
- Neglected your appearance at work

You must take ownership of your situation – your career, your life, your thoughts – and dominate it. In this competitive job market and fast-paced business world, you need to update yourself on new technologies, acquire new skills, and understand new processes. Also, stay positive and surround yourself with people who make you feel good about yourself. Change your routine every now and then. If you are in a vicious cycle of waking up, going to work, and going to bed, then switch up your routine: Go for a walk during lunchtime, meet your coworkers or friends for lunch, go to happy hour with close friends who can relate to your situation, or work out after work. However, do not do too many things or spread yourself too thin.

Boredom

When you do the same thing for years, day in and day out, you might feel as if you're stuck in a dead-end job – but you need not go through life this way. Although you may need the salary to pay the bills, being miserable isn't worth this sacrifice.

If you are bored at your job, it has probably become too easy for you, so volunteer to gain new responsibilities, which can help to bring excitement to your job. In addition to refreshing your current position, volunteering at your favorite charity can open new doors for you. Also, to help make your full-time tolerable or even more enjoyable, consider getting a part-time job in an area that interests you so you are at least doing something you like *part-time*. Working at a part-time job in the area you are passionate about allows you to tolerate your current job and slowly build on your passion at your part-time job, where you might eventually become full-time.

You might get bored if you are still doing your job as you did it several years ago, so mix things up. If you normally eat lunch in your office or cafeteria and your workplace has benches outside, have lunch outside. Take a walk during lunchtime. If your job is boring, think of ways to challenge yourself: Find new ways to do the exact same task, or try working at different times or taking different shifts.

Procrastination

Procrastination affects your professional career and reputation. If you procrastinate at work, your coworkers and boss might lose confidence in you because they can't rely on you to get your work done. You can ask yourself the following questions to help identify when you may be procrastinating:

- Do you fill your workday with meaningless tasks?
- Do you read your emails one by one, as they come into your inbox, or do you read them several times daily without responding to them? Constantly checking your emails and responding to them every time they come in takes more time versus checking your email two or three times a day and responding to them.

- Before starting a priority task, do you immediately take a coffee break?
- Do you leave a high-priority task on your to-do list for several days or weeks?
- Do you wait to be in the "right" mood or time to complete a task?

Some reasons for procrastination include:
- Job dissatisfaction: By completing only the easy tasks, procrastinators can focus on the pleasant aspects of their jobs.
- Disorganization or boredom
- Lack of information or resources: You may doubt you have the skills or resources needed, so you seek comfort in doing tasks you know you can complete. Unfortunately, the big task will not go away.
- Fear of success: You may also fear success as much as you fear failure, thinking that success will leave you swamped with more requests, or that you will be pushed to take on things you feel are beyond your skills and knowledge.
- Feeling of becoming overwhelmed.

Procrastination is a concern because employees who fail to pay attention to details and instead rush through their work make mistakes and/or miss deadlines. If you identify why you procrastinate, then you can try to fix the problem.

The more you do at or outside of work, the harder it is for you to get bored and become complacent. The possibilities are endless, but you have to be proactive. There are always opportunities to form a meaningful connection to your work. Through soul searching, introspection, planning, action, and proper support, you can redirect your career, incorporating into your life what excites, invigorates, and makes you feel good about yourself.

Challenge yourself by setting achievable goals. You never know: You might even have fun!

Chapter 3
Resuscitation

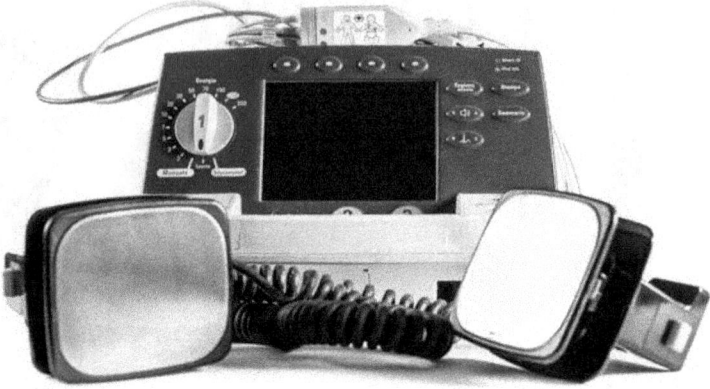

Deep Breathing

There are strategies to help breathe new life into a job or career: In addition to defining your purpose and identifying your passion, you can generate a renewed feeling of excitement in your job by making learning and development an annual goal. The amount of learning you do every day in your job helps resuscitate a flat-lined career.

Self-Reflection: A Look Inside

Like a car, we have an indicator system, which is our gut feeling or intuition. A car's indicator system warns the driver of impending issues, such as the oil indicator light meaning that we should check the oil. These indicators provide guidance when something feels wrong or uncoordinated. When we pay attention to these indicators, our car will remain in good operating condition. The same is true about us: When we feel uncomfortable or lack of inner peace, our indicator tells us we need to reevaluate our circumstances. The most dangerous thing anyone can do is to continue on a path not in alignment with honesty and self-authenticity.

Live a life and work in a profession based on your desires and expectations, not those of others. Be courageous by being honest with yourself, which may require that you inconvenience yourself, disrupt your routine, or do things that are uncomfortable – but being honest with yourself can make you stronger.

Sometimes situations happen to provide you with opportunities to be honest with yourself. If you are unhappy, have the courage to face your own convictions and identify what you are feeling and why. We have all faced a "moment of truth." This can mean we are coming to conclusions or decisions that may be life-altering.

Each situation is of consequence, as it usually involves self-discovery and the truth about our beliefs. When you have an opportunity to be honest with yourself, you might have to change jobs, end a relationship, or decide the next path to take. Although a sometimes difficult process, taking responsibility for your professional development can be exciting and rewarding.

According to the article "Willingness to be Honest with Yourself" by Blue Ninja, being authentic with yourself allows you to have honest relationships. If we are genuine, others are more likely to respect us, which contributes to our experiencing inner peace. Honesty and integrity are great personal attributes that build great personal and professional relationships. The overall message for all of us is to stand firm in what we believe and to be honest with ourselves. We cannot fully treat others with respect until we respect ourselves and stand in our power. This means having integrity and owning the responsibility that comes with every decision we make.

Be sure to practice listening to your intuition. If you constantly feel a lack of peace or believe you should make an important decision, take action.

A Powerful Remedy

Your success (or lack thereof) is a result of your actions, behaviors, and choices. While outside conditions may cause you to change your plans, you own your own success or failure.

The first step to owning your success is self-empowerment by which you grant yourself the power to succeed. If you believe you can be successful at something, you will be. Through self-empowerment, you take the actions and risks to achieve your career goals and get what you want.

Only *you* can decide what type of employee you are. Are you a clock watcher or an engaged employee? A clock-watcher employee drags through the workday, watching the clock and concerned about the next break, lunchtime, and leaving. The clock-watcher despises Mondays and often laments how long Friday takes to arrive. An engaged (successful) employee is proactive and learns as much as possible about their job. They become subject-matter experts whom others seek and who are available to help whenever and wherever needed. The company, their supervisor, and team members can rely on their support.

Empower yourself by stepping outside your comfort zone and being proactive. Ninety-percent of what you believe determines your success. Being accountable for your actions and learning from experiences will help you develop a better plan for success.

Chapter 4
Growth and Development Chart

Jump-Starting Your Career

The following are summarized strategies to jump-start or restore your career:

- Always be honest with yourself and others.
- Become a better communicator.
- Maintain a positive attitude.
- Exhibit flexibility.
- Be a problem-solver.
- Treat others with respect, and be supportive.

Exercising Your Options

According to the U.S. Bureau of Labor Statistics, the average person born in the latter years of the baby boom (1957–1964) held 11.3 jobs from age 18 to age 46, and nearly half of these jobs were held from ages 18 to 24.

To advance your career, figure out what you want to do, where you want to work, and where you want to live. For example, what do you want out of your career? Do you want to be VP of Nursing? Head of an

IT department? Manager of a mid- to large-scale business or of your own company? Developer of an award-winning app? Know who and what you are, and build on that information.

For some people, focusing on only one career path is difficult. Unless you plan to go back to school, be careful setting a goal to become a network security master if you have spent your entire career as a nurse. Do not focus on something you do not fully believe you can achieve. That does not mean you have to play everything safe: You still must take risks, but make sure those risks will help you achieve your goals. Once you decide on your career destination, create a realistic plan of action to help you achieve your career goals.

When looking for another job, whether it's outside your organization or a transfer within your current organization, do not share your job search with anyone outside of your immediate trusted circle of family and friends. That is, don't share this information with your coworkers until *after* you have the job offer letter. It has been my experience that if you share this information with the wrong person, that person might tell someone else, who might talk negatively about you – or he or she might apply for the job and get it – and you'll lose that job opportunity!

Conducting Research

If interested in working for a firm, visit its website career opportunities section, which includes open positions. Also visit the Human Resources page, where you'll find information about employee benefits. Even if you don't find a position that matches your current expertise and skills, some company websites will allow you to submit your resume and cover letter for future consideration. Be sure to research the company as much as possible:

- Use the public library or local bookstore to locate and read information about the company/organization.
- Access books, journals, magazines, newspapers, and any reference materials useful for investors and job seekers.
- Ask the reference librarian about connections to investor online publications or services, such as Value Line or Lexis-Nexis.
- Read and/or check online resources for major business publications, e.g., *Forbes, Money, Kiplinger's, The Wall Street Journal,* or *Investor's Business Daily.*
- Go online to the company's website and their competitors' sites.

- Use investor and news websites to learn what is happening in the news with this company and its competitors.
- Consult Bizjournals.com, a good resource for finding information by industry and location.

Assessing Your Skills

Most organizations are fast-paced and constantly changing: From new technology and techniques to new trends and emerging markets, staying current is essential if you want to remain competitive. Unfortunately, most companies today are preoccupied with developing new strategies to continue to grow and thrive and less time encouraging their *staff* to grow and thrive, so their employees are forced to find alternative learning solutions.

Oftentimes, you are responsible for finding your own career path and acquiring relevant skills, so change with the times, keep up with new technology, learn new skills, or enhance old skills.

Matching your strengths and talents with the needs of potential employers takes time. As you scan multiple resources for the ideal job, focus on descriptions that match your skill set, not just your interests. In a tough job market, employers may not consider an applicant whose skills do not meet their specific hiring criteria. If the job description states that candidates must have a working knowledge of PowerPoint, apply only if you have PowerPoint presentation knowledge. However, job descriptions often list preferences, such as "a working knowledge of PowerPoint a plus," which means you can still apply without having that skill. Still, you will be more successful if you have PowerPoint knowledge.

When you're unemployed or fear a layoff, conducting a self-assessment is essential – and should be done annually. During this annual assessment, evaluate current skills, talents, abilities, strengths, weaknesses, interests, and work values. In addition, re-examine your accomplishments and achievements, particularly those that may be suitable to a prospective employer.

For example, if you are a registered nurse and your goal is to become a nurse manager or director, you must obtain an advanced degree, so seek counsel from another nurse who has obtained an advanced degree or a nurse coordinator in your unit, and volunteer for projects that improve patient care. If you are an accountant who wants to become an investment banker, you might have some skills that overlap, but you will need an in-depth knowledge of the stock markets and tax regulations. The same applies if you are a web designer entrepreneur and want new clients: Keep your skills updated and learn marketing skills. If you are a food server who desires to become a chef, learn as much as you can about those requirements.

If you are an accountant who prepares financial information, continue to update your knowledge about the latest accounting software. If you are a web designer, learn about the latest web development tools and Internet trends. If you work in the hospitality industry, stay informed about the latest safety and hygiene requirements. If you are a nurse, attend continuing education classes and conferences to stay updated on current trends in the industry. Check trade magazines, professional organizations, and websites, where you can get current information.

There are many resources to help determine skills and expertise for careers, such as the *NYU Wagner Tracks Exercise Guide*, also a great tool to help you map your career.

In "Don't Stand Still: Why You Need to Take Charge of Your Own Professional Development," Gary Swart identifies four strategies to use to stretch yourself beyond your comfort zone:

1. **"Go beyond your comfort zone...**Take on more responsibility than you think you can handle...whatever happens, you'll be strong and wiser for the experience."

2. **"Surround yourself with people you can learn from.** If you need to immerse yourself in a new topic or area, there's no faster way to do this than to spend time with people who are already experts."

3. **"Read as much as you can.**

4. **"Don't forget to cultivate your social network**...ensure you also network outside of work to meet people with a wider range of backgrounds..."

Does your career path require specialized training, such as that required to become an attorney or neurosurgeon? If so, seek opportunities to learn as much about your field as possible by talking with those already practicing the profession.

Most companies offer mentorships and professional development courses. Take an online course or sign up for classes at a local school to expand your knowledge base and increase your marketability, as well as boost your resume and career, which may impress the higher-ups. If you are self-employed, you can offer more to clients and increase your earning potential by having a course or two under your belt. Attend an educational institution that offers weekend, evening, and online classes, or industry conferences and seminars. Ask your coworkers and supervisor about opportunities for you to learn new skills.

Improve your skills and expertise by volunteering. Many nonprofit companies will welcome your expertise, knowledge, and skills, providing you with additional experience to include in your resume.

A friend and former colleague often shared that we all must be prepared in the workplace, continuously updating our education and skills if we want to reach our career goals, so make a list of the knowledge, skills, and expertise required for the position you have or want. If you do not have what is required, return to school or read industry trade magazines. Once you have identified the skills needed for advancement, evaluate which skills are the best for your current career path and take the steps to acquire them.

If interested in advancing your career and obtaining a more senior position, you need to do more than just show up to work every day and meet basic job requirements: To be competitive, you must be proactive and acquire additional skills and experience. Research indicates we have an innate desire for achievement and psychological growth. Employees want to learn new things and master new skills, which enables them to make more of an impact.

Today's job market is turbulent and competitive, so take action to continuously develop and update your skills. By investing in your skill set and cultivating a solid online reputation through social media, you prepare yourself for any opportunity that might arise.

Continuing Education

Invest in yourself with continuing education, a great way to stay abreast of the latest industry rules and regulations, as it provides you with new and improved products and planning techniques. Requirements to obtain continuing education can be easily acquired via the Internet through approved online CE providers like WebCE and RegEd, which offer easy, accessible, and relevant courses.

If you do not invest in yourself, you have no stake in the professional development game and might become invisible. I am not suggesting you go crazy, like me, by obtaining two master's degrees and six certifications in six areas. However, continue educating yourself to develop your career, as the next new hire on your team can show up with excellent credentials or skills and want your job.

If you owned your own business, you would do everything you could to make sure it succeeds. You would probably spend time marketing yourself and learning ways to improve your efficiency. The same is true if you work for someone else.

Contract Work

You can also boost your career, gain experience, and make a little money on the side by accepting freelance and contract work. Whether this is your main source of income or moonlighting work, contract work gives you the chance to challenge yourself with new projects, expand your professional network, and support your lifestyle.

However, be careful when doing contract work: Make sure there is no conflict of interest or not to break nondisclosure agreements. Before advertising for a side gig, check the employee manual at your current workplace. Sometimes contracts disallow employees from working for competitors or competing directly for business. If you write web copy at work and advertise your services as a contract or freelance worker, your company could see that as competition. If you work at a hospital and start a home care agency, there may be a conflict of interest.

Your Medicine Cabinet

Always keep an updated list of your accomplishments in an electronic file, e.g., an Excel spreadsheet. Also, keep a manual folder that includes:
- magazine articles
- congratulatory letters
- kudos from your supervisor, clients, and customers
- annual performance evaluations
- descriptions of successful activities

We live very busy lives and often forget to keep records of notable successes.

Evaluating Goals

"If you fail to plan, you are planning to fail!"
—Benjamin Franklin
Leading author, printer, political theorist, politician, freemason, postmaster, scientist

For most people, creating goals is easy, but applying themselves to execute them is a struggle. Turn your dreams into goals you can accomplish, and ensure you reach the finish line by following these suggestions:

1. **Write down your goals, and display them. A study shows that** 76% of those who wrote down goals with actionable commitments they put into weekly progress reports and shared with friends actually accomplished their goals. In contrast, only 43% of those in a control group who did *not* write down their goals accomplished their objectives and had a high stress level. Writing down your goals makes them real: They are tangible words on paper, not dreams in your mind. Goal setting helps employees focus on skill gaps between their current abilities and those they need to acquire to succeed at the next level. Ongoing training opportunities fill these gaps, as they improve opportunities for promotion and give employees more satisfaction for and engagement in their work.

2. **Break big goals down into smaller ones.** Break goals down into manageable weekly and daily actionable bites. If you don't, you might lose motivation if the goal seems far away or too big to accomplish.

3. **Make an action plan and follow it.** The best gift you can give yourself is a well-thought-out action plan. Organize your smaller daily and weekly goals in one place so you can easily check your progress or send it to others so that they can hold you accountable.

4. **Work on your goals as early in the day as possible.** If you study successful people, you will find that, most of the time, they do more before the sun rises than the rest of the world does in a day. Work on your goals the first thing in the morning so you can feel as if you have started your day right.

5. **Tell others your goals to keep you accountable.** Find a coach,

good friend, or mentor who will take on the role of motivator and occasional butt-kicker. When you know that someone will check your progress, you have a greater tendency to follow through on your goals. You will come to value this service immensely when you see your efficiency and effectiveness improve.

6. **Make sure your goals excite you.** Your goals should be a source of joy in your life and one of the main reasons you get out of bed in the morning. If your goals do not excite you, you need to re-evaluate them.

7. **Use positive language in your goals.** Setting and accomplishing your goals changes you: You become a positive person who is more excited about life. No one can get passionate about going through the day trying to defeat negativity. For example, do not say, "My goal is not to mess up today"; instead, use positive language: "My goal is to excel today in my career by doing X, Y, and Z." Spend your day chasing and catching success.

8. **Set goals in multiple life areas.** Do not reserve your goals only for your career: Challenge yourself to set goals in fitness, finance, family, relationships, educational, spirituality, health, and adventure. You can improve every area of your life by attaching a goal to it.

9. **Set performance versus outcome goals.** Many events are outside of your control. For example, you may have a bucket list goal to run a 26-mile marathon, follow an action plan, and train daily, and even though you are ready to run the marathon, a huge storm temporarily postpones the event. The weather is out of your control. You met all your performance goals and were prepared, but life happened, so you could not run the marathon that day. Regardless of the outcome, you became the person who *can* run a 26-mile marathon.

When you set your goals, do not say, "My goal is to run a 26-mile marathon by January 2018." Instead say, "My goal is to be completely prepared to run a 26-mile marathon by January 2018 and to do all that is within my power." The first goal is attainable, as it depends solely on you; the second goal is only attainable if everything works out perfectly, e.g., as no bad weather or travel delays, etc.

> "In the absence of clearly defined goals, we become strangely loyal to performing daily trivia until ultimately we become enslaved by it."
> —Robert Heinlein, American science-fiction writer

So what are you aiming for? If your answer is "nothing," then you probably will not like what you get out of this life. Instead of simply drifting along, reacting to whatever life brings you, *try to create the future you want.* While we cannot control *everything* that happens to us, we *can* control *some* of what happens to us by following goals that bring out our passion for life.

> "If you want to live a happy life, tie it to a goal, not to people or things."
> —Albert Einstein, German-born theoretical physicist who developed the general theory of relativity

The following strategies may help ensure that you successfully execute a successful career path:

1. **Establish a professional development plan.** Some people have their career goal in mind but have not prepared a path to get there. The first step is for you to establish a professional development plan to prepare yourself for the position you want. Develop your plan well in advance. For example, if you want to be a senior executive, you might have to have 10 to 15 years of pertinent experience, so you need to plan to achieve this goal.

2. **Identify areas for professional growth.** To know where you are going, you must first understand where you have been. Self-reflection and discipline are keys to career advancement. People who identify their strengths and areas for improvement can make informed decisions in the next steps of their career plan. Input must be objective, so involve others who know you. By taking these necessary and specific steps, you can position and prepare yourself for future opportunities.

3. **Consider professional associations, memberships, and certifications.** With rapid changes in the workplace and a

continuing climate of consolidation, the job market is more challenging than ever. Becoming a member of a group or getting certified in a skill is a mark of excellence that separates you from the crowd and serves as a vital networking tool enabling you to make connections throughout the industry.

4. **Align your career path with your goal.** Having a depth and wealth of experience is important. Proactively develop a career map, working in the trenches to gain insight and knowledge in numerous areas. You need a record of accomplishment of measurable outcomes along your journey to demonstrate leadership in your career.

5. **Identify the organization where you would like to work.** Hiring organizations and individuals want to know your motivation, so do your homework. Research the organization, leadership team members, and community to gather important information. Be prepared to answer questions like, "Why do you want to work here?" "Why do you want to live in this area?" "What are your ties to this organization?"

6. **Align organizational culture with personal values.** Recognizing cultural fit determines your career success. Reflect on your personal values, and identify your ideal organizational culture. Would you prefer to work for a for-profit or not-for-profit organization? Organizations seek individuals who share their mission and values. Knowing what you represent will help identify cultural fit and ensure a successful partnership.

Emergency Kit

Today's job seekers have many options for finding available jobs. Below are a few popular job search tools you can use during your job search:

1. **Newspapers and craigslist.** Local newspapers and craigslist provide listings for available positions in your area. For example, the newspaper classified ads may include jobs posted by the local employment commission, and jobs listed on craigslist aren't included in any aggregator sites, such as Indeed.com. A word of caution about craigslist ads: Please be aware that these ads are free to post, so some listings may not be legitimate.

2. **Online Aggregators.** Online job aggregators collect job postings from across the Internet. Postings are combined into one database that job seekers can use to search positions by title, employer, keyword, location, and other metrics. Aggregators like SimplyHired.com and Indeed.com include postings from employer websites and jobs posted on large career sites, e.g., Monster.com and CareerBuilder.com.

3. **Specialized Industry Sites/Publications.** Conducting an Internet search for industry-specific jobs can help you find the right employer and the right job. Some websites and publications provide specific industry information:
   - wallstjobs.com for financial careers
   - dice.com for tech jobs
   - marketingjobs.com for marketing professionals

   These sites also allow you to search for positions and post your resume so that potential employers can find you.

4. **Headhunters or Recruiters?** A headhunter, or recruiter, provides employment recruiting services and can help match qualified candidates with specific career opportunities. Headhunters typically work for a corporation to find talent and may have a pool of candidates from which to select. Most established professionals work with headhunters and are looking for a specific job and salary. A good recruiter will have connections within your industry and help you refine your resume and cover letter.

5. **Job and Career Fairs.** You can find information about upcoming job and career fairs through your local career centers, state and local government websites, private companies, and Internet searches. Job and career fairs provide you with opportunities to meet potential employer face to face. You can gather information about these employers to determine if a company you are setting your sights on is a good fit. Employers will have recruiters available to answer questions, accept resumes, meet with the potential candidates, and possibly conduct mini-interviews. Dress professionally, and bring an updated resume specific to the position for which you are

interviewing.

6. **Social Media.** As a professional, you must protect your professional reputation, so it's not a good idea to share, on social media, photos of you attending wild drinking parties. If you have posted a few pictures in the past you are not proud of, fix the situation by cleaning up your social media profile *today*, as you *must* present yourself as a professional.

   Depending on your skills, employers may also contact you and other potential candidates by searching social media sites like LinkedIn, Twitter, Facebook, Instagram, and Google Plus. So dedicate time to scrutinizing your social media pages and creating a professional, up-to-date, and compelling online presence, as your online presence can help you gain an edge in today's competitive job market and make a huge difference as to whether or not a potential employer decides to call you.

   Remember: Social media may be the first interaction others have with you. Make a good first impression, or risk stunting your career growth. Also, ensure your social media accounts are the same and consistent so that prospective customers or employers can find you. You never know who is reviewing your social media profile.

7. **Resumes.** According to editor, proofreader, and resume writer Hallie Belt of www.beltstyles.com, be sure to have a well-written, updated resume on hand. Even when the companies are not looking to hire during the hiring freeze, they are always keeping an eye out for the best, most talented people.

   After submitting your resume, be prepared to discuss supplemental experiences the employer might find important. Search the Internet for interview preparation tools, e.g., a job interview prep sheet, to help you focus on experiences you believe are applicable and match the employer's needs.

8. **Cover Letters.** Belt also suggests that you keep your cover letter short, tailoring it to each job. Explain how your skills knowledge can benefit a potential employer. Show you helped the companies you worked for and how your skills will help your potential employer.

9. **LinkedIn Page.** According to Belt, keep your LinkedIn page updated, insert all of your skills, and make it a skeletal version of your resume.

10. **Business Cards.** Keep your business cards current and handy, as you never know where you might meet a potential employer or contact.

Networking: Nurse's Advice

What separates people who are satisfied with their career from people who aren't? Those with a satisfying career might be involved in networking, a great strategy to nurse and advance a career no matter what the career direction is.

In today's job market, it is important to be a good networker. As you progress in your field or hope to advance to a managerial or leadership position, the competition for jobs will become strong, so having a strong network behind you can help set you apart, as well as help you take those next steps. Build relationships beyond your immediate team and network with company colleagues, mentors, and customers. These individuals will help advance your career. *Remember: People* are your career's greatest asset.

You need not search for a new job to build a network of business contacts. Network inside and outside of your job, always building and maintaining your network of business contacts. Make it your intention to build positive relationships and stay connected to former colleagues and clients. Doing this helps you to find new opportunities. As a matter of fact, a former coworker recommended me for my current position. The following are some ways to network:

1. **Become a member of a professional organization.** Many people find their next job through networking, so always be courteous and professional, whether you are networking in person, via email, or online. If you make a new contact, ask if you can stay in touch. To broaden your network, join professional organizations like the Rotary Club, Toastmasters, or Project Management Institute, and be sure to keep your business cards current so you can hand them out. Networking involves being proactive: Attend networking events, make phone calls, and use social media to share your expertise,

knowledge, and skills.

I cannot stress enough the importance of networking, and simply being available is the key to networking and building business relationships in any industry. By maintaining professional social networking profiles, talking to others in your industry, and attending networking events, you increase your chances of forging solid connections that can boost your career. Get your name out there, and make sure those in your industry know who you are.

2. **Contact business associates, friends, and relatives.** Since many employers rely heavily on employee referrals, ask your business associates, friends, and relatives if they could recommend you for positions they know are available so that you can increase job leads. Companies like to know whom they're hiring, so if you and the company have a contact in common, you might have a greater chance of getting a job there than you would if you aren't a "known" entity.

3. **Connect with alumni.** Most colleges and universities have alumni associations that also have an online presence. If you have not already done so, join your college or university's alumni association (you will probably have to create an online account). Joining an alumni association is a wonderful opportunity to display your accomplishments, expertise, knowledge, and skills – and you will be able to network virtually with alumni in the U.S. and around the world. If your college offers a searchable online database, search by company name.

Once you have established your alumni account, contact any alumni who work for that company. Choose the most recent graduates, as they are more familiar with the interview and hiring process and can also share their early, on-the-job experiences. Also, connect with older alumni, since they may have inside information on available positions and share information about corporate culture, history, and career paths.

Attend alumni networking events, where you can rekindle old connections and make new ones. Always make it your goal to leave any networking meeting with at least two to five new contacts.

As you advance in your career, you will build a network of professionals you can turn to for anything – from the latest industry news to career advice. Alumni contacts are valuable for their insights, as well as their connections.

4. **Get involved in your industry's professional association.** For example, if you are a nurse, join professional nursing associations. There are hundreds of groups out there for different industries: those for student nurses, local nursing organizations, nursing specialties, etc., so ask your colleagues or manager which ones they would recommend. The goal is to join a few organizations that align with either your status or future career aspirations. You may get a lot out of these affiliations if they have formal and informal networking events, virtual chat, message boards, and other resources for getting to know others in your field. You may also get discounts on continuing education seminars and courses in a nursing career, where there are many professional paths to explore. Networking can be especially helpful for finding out about new positions, meeting mentors, learning about interesting industry events, and exploring other development opportunities.

   Networking through a professional association is also a great way to make personal connections and build relationships with other professionals who can relate to your profession: You can share tips and advice, lean on each other for support, and commiserate. If your job takes a physical and/or emotional toll on you, fellow workers in the same industry will probably be able relate to you.

5. **Cultivate relationships.** While professional associations are a good start for meeting others in your profession, the anchor of your network will come from you and what you do. Cultivating relationships with the people you meet in school, on the job, and in your personal life can help you out. As a college student, you can start building your network by exchanging contact information with those you meet. Keep in touch on social media or through email – and remember that nothing beats in-person networking, so attend conferences and events, strike up

conversations, and exchange business cards with the people you meet. If you work for a large company, try to attend social mixers or company-sponsored events. At these types of events, I have met many staff members who later became my team members on different projects.

6. **Use social media.** It is understandable that, with a full-time job, you will not have much time to dedicate to in-person networking, so using social media and online networking might benefit you. Ensure you have a complete and updated profile on LinkedIn, the most obvious networking platform, as it is strictly for professionals. Keep in touch with colleagues, working friends, and other people in your industry. You can also join industry-based LinkedIn groups to discuss trends and best practices, as well as follow the company pages of your industry organizations. Another way to keep your account active is to share an interesting article about your profession on your page, or comment on information that other people share.

Beyond LinkedIn, the lines between personal and professional connections are blurred on Facebook and Twitter. Even if you follow mostly friends and family, try not to post anything you would regret if your colleagues or supervisors saw it, and do *not* post anything specific about your job. Your connections on all these platforms can help you professionally: An acquaintance can refer you to a job you did not know about, or you might find out about your school's alumni events.

Besides Facebook and Twitter, there are many job-specific online communities you can join, many of which are free. They may offer articles, blogs, email newsletters, forums, and/or other tools to keep you informed, and give you a way to communicate with other members.

7. **Contact people you already know.** Leverage your current relationships to find entry points into your new field. All it takes is a different type of conversation to get started. Ask your contacts what they know and whom they know in the field that interests you. Follow up on their leads, and you will quickly make progress.

Finally, as busy as you might be, try to make time for

networking. Whether you spend a few minutes updating your social profiles or commit to attending a couple of conferences each year, consider this energy you spend a wise investment in yourself.

Networking Do's and Don'ts

As mentioned before, we don't attend networking events solely to make business connections, pass out business cards, and get a job: We need to take time and have real conversations with people at the event, but do not be aggressive while social networking or when following up with those you meet.

When you attend networking events, focus on building relationships by getting to know people and *then* getting their business cards. People may not buy your products or services today, or they may not seem to be a good fit for your career goals, but they may know (and send your way) numerous people who need your products or services. Therefore, developing those relationships is most important. If possible, write key words on the back of their business card as a reminder of what you discussed. Quality is far more important than quantity. Make sure you have made enough personal connections that people remember you when you call later or see them the next time.

It is okay to talk about what you do or share your career goals, the problems you solve, and outcomes your clients get, but be careful about assuming those you speak with at the networking event can help you with your career goals.

Do not ask about job openings or solicit work by asking if they need your products or services. If the person you are talking to is interested in helping you or your services, schedule an appointment or meet for coffee. You will be much more likely to make a connection or the sale after you have established a relationship.

Networking Bedside Manner

Whether you are networking in person or online, try to be generous to others and give more than you get. Help others who might be looking for job leads. Endorse coworkers, and share articles and posts from someone you admire in the industry, or posts from your employer. People will notice your goodwill, which might open doors for you. Being kind and supportive to others in your network will come back to you someday when you need support.

Networking in person is about being genuine and authentic, building trust and relationships, and seeing how you can help others. Try to strike up a conversation, even if you know no one in the room. This can be challenging if you are on the shy side, but the more you practice introducing yourself, the easier it will get.

Before joining a network group, visit as many groups as possible. Many groups will allow you to visit up to two times or more before joining them. During the event, pay attention to the tone and attitude of the group. Do you observe people being supportive of one another? Do you like the leadership's style, and does the leader appear competent? Once you join, volunteer for different positions in the group – a great way to stay visible. Additionally, give back to groups that have the potential to help you.

You want to be perceived as a powerful resource for others. You may offer to do a presentation that would be helpful to the group. If you are known as a strong resource, people remember to turn to you for suggestions, ideas, referrals, etc. Have a clear understanding of what you do, why, and for whom, as well as what makes you special or different from others doing the same thing. To get referrals, you must clearly understand what you do and easily articulate it to others.

Follow through on referrals as soon as possible. When people give you referrals, your actions are a reflection on them, so be sure to follow up promptly with any connection you make at the network events, as well as on the referrals made to you out of respect to the person who gave you the referrals. For example, if I referred my friend to my manager for an open position, my friend's professional behavior and performance would be a reflection on me because I referred her. Respect and honor those who send you referrals, and your referrals will grow.

Finally, call those you meet who may benefit from what you do. Express that you enjoyed meeting them and ask if you could get together to share ideas. Remember: Do *not* try to sell them whatever services or products you have, and do *not* try to get them to hire you; instead, use this time to learn from them and their experiences.

Chapter 5
"The Doctor Will See You Now"

Job Interview Prep

Prepare for the job interview. Whether you get the job or not, interviewing is a skill that you must hone through preparation and practice, which will reflect positively on you during the interview and can make a difference between your getting an acceptance or rejection letter. Lack of preparation is one of the biggest interview errors that job seekers can make, so assess the skills, interests, values, and accomplishments documented on your resume, and do the following:

- Research the targeted industry, company, and position.
- Develop and practice answering typical and targeted interview questions. These questions should reflect your research on the company and position and never include questions whose answers are readily available in the company literature or website. Quintessential Careers suggests answering the "Basic 3" practice interview questions:
    - Why are you interested in this field?
    - Why are you interested in this company?

o Why are you interested in this position?
Be prepared to discuss and answer questions about your resume:
   o Your greatest weakness or your lack of related experience
   o Your lack of leadership experiences
   o Your record of job-hopping

Practice your interviewing skills. Once you have prepared for the job interview, you must practice your interview skills. Ask a family member, friend, career counselor, or career coach to help you. You can also practice in front of a mirror or video: Record yourself responding to interview questions. Audiotape your answers, and listen to them at home and on your way to the interview. While reviewing the video and the audio, listen for inflections of your voice and watch your body language, particularly your gestures, facial expressions, poise, energy, and enthusiasm in your answers. Ask yourself how you can improve, enhance, develop, or revise your answers and/or delivery.

Interviewing requires advanced skills, and you can improve with practice. Most college and university career services offer mock interviews and interview workshops. Always ask for genuine feedback to help you identify areas of improvement. Practice helps reduce fear and nervousness.

Keeping Up Appearances
Prepare your clothes and appearance.
- Select appropriate attire at least a day before the interview. Be familiar with the organization's culture, and dress accordingly. Unless the interviewer states a specific and different dress code, always dress in business attire.
- Make sure clothing is free of wrinkles, lint, etc.
- Avoid wearing perfumes or colognes.
- Do a test-run to determine comfort level: Skirts/Dresses that are too short and shirts/pants that are too tight may cause you or others to be distracted or uncomfortable.
- Minimize accessories. *Remember: Less is more.* Be memorable for the right reasons.

Be sure to bring the right tools.
- Extra copies of your resume in a folder

- Your portfolio
- A small notebook to take notes, but keep note-taking to a minimum so as not to distract either you or the interviewer(s)
- A nice briefcase or purse to hold documents

Know the interview location.
- If possible, drive by the location of the company before the interview.
- Plan to arrive at the designated office 30 minutes in advance. Allow ample time for traffic, the chance of getting lost, and parking difficulties.

The Interview: Being Your Own Advocate
- **Sit up straight and lean in.** Although feeling a little anxious at the interview is helpful to maintain a level of alertness, if you feel unusually anxious, sit up straight and lean slightly toward the interviewer to help you find a balance between poise/calm and energy/enthusiasm.
- **State your case effectively.** Be sure you have strong, valid reasons to change careers. If you know why you want to make the change and what you stand to gain from it, you will increase your odds of success considerably. Also, be sure you can articulate those reasons to potential employers and explain what is in it for them.
- **Focus on what you do for the company**. You want the interviewers to remember you above other candidates. Everything about the job interview should focus on how you can help the company, what *you* bring to the position, and why the employer should hire *you*! The interview may be your only opportunity to make a positive, lasting impression, so treat it with care.
- **Collect business cards.** Be sure to collect business cards from every interviewer. If they do not have business cards available, write down their contact information and email address.
- **Ask about time frames.** Find out the time frame for filling the position, how and when you will be notified, and if the interviewers would like additional information or materials from you.
- **Remember:** Do not ask about salary or benefits until a job offer has been made.

Follow-up Appointment

After the interview, follow up with the interviewer by using these protocols:

- **Send an email thank-you note.** Within 48 hours of your interview, send a thank-you email note to every person who interviewed you. Keep it short and simple (only 2 to 3 sentences).
- **Send a *handwritten* thank-you note.** Be sure to thank each interviewer for his or her time, reiterating your interest in *and* emphasizing your specific qualifications for the position.

Once you are hired, learn all you can about your new position. Become a subject matter expert at your job. If you are already familiar with the job, you are ahead of the game and on your way to even greater success.

Life-Altering Event

Sometimes, a new career opportunity is an honor. Timing is everything, and accepting the right opportunity can turn your career around. For example, a job transfer can open up an entirely new world to you and your career. Be fearless, ready, and willing to try new and different tasks or opportunities. There is no easy career switch you can click to breathe life into your job. However, accepting every opportunity is not always a good choice, so you must learn when decline down an opportunity.

Chapter 6
Stress

Stress affects millions of people. One of the most common forms of stress is related to our careers and the workplace. Many people flat-line their career at the first sign of stress, job challenge, or another type of job-related struggle. They want to quit their job or give up the minute they start to experience job stress.

A 2008 American Psychological Association survey indicated that more than one third of American workers experience chronic work stress, costing American businesses billions of dollars a year in lost work hours and medical bills. All the worrying at work can have serious consequences on the quality of your personal and professional life. In today's economic difficulty, work-related stress is more common than ever. Employees worry about whether they can keep their job, their health insurance, and even their homes.

When someone experiences stress, they exhibit physical and

emotional signs and symptoms. Depending on the level and frequency, stress can lead to serious problems. The heart rate increases, headaches can develop, and often, people become irritated more easily.

Americans are overworked and stressed out. Our fast-paced lifestyles are wearing us out. Persistent uncertainty about the economy is paralyzing us. Fear is our common response. Our fast-paced lifestyles are wearing us out. Persistent uncertainty about the economy is paralyzing us. Fear is our common response.

The U.S. is becoming a nation of nervous wrecks, and our lifestyle has something to do with this problem: We do not value free time and leisure as much as other cultures do. In America, we work longer hours, with fewer breaks than almost any other developed nation. In Africa, it is part of our culture to take midday afternoon naps. Even industrial powerhouses, like Germany and France, have 35-hour workweeks, but their productivity levels are among the highest in the world. On average, people there may have lower income rates, but their standard of living and quality of life are above that of the U.S.

Americans are also anxiety-ridden. The American Psychiatric Association found that between 2 percent and 4 percent of Americans suffer from anxiety disorder. By 2009, follow-up studies showed a dramatic rise to 49.5 percent. That means 117 million U.S. citizens are affected by disabling anxiety at least once in their lives. For the first time, prescriptions for medications against anxiety and depression outrank all others, including drugs to lower cholesterol and blood pressure, according to the latest reports on spending for health care in the U.S.

Diagnosing Stress

Then identify your stress triggers. When and under what circumstances does stress affect us most? Some causes of stress are easy to identify, such as job pressures, relationship problems, or financial difficulties. However, daily hassles and demands, such as commuting, arranging childcare, or overcommitting at work, also can contribute to your stress level.

Positive events also can be stressful. You can experience high stress levels if, in the same year, you get married, start a new job, and buy a new house. Negative life events are more stressful. That is why it is important to assess the positive changes in your life. Once you have identified your stress triggers, you can think about strategies for dealing with them. Identifying what aspect of the situation you can control is a good starting point.

Warning Signs

When you feel overwhelmed at work, you might lose confidence and even become irritable or withdrawn. This can make you less productive and less effective in your job, which can make the work seem less rewarding. Ignoring the warning signs of work stress can lead to bigger problems. Beyond interfering with job performance and satisfaction, chronic or intense stress can lead to physical and emotional health problems.

Symptoms of workplace stress. You are suffering from workplace stress if you if you are experiencing some or all of the following:
- feel increasingly cynical at work
- work in a chaotic, high-stress, or dangerous environment
- believe your job doesn't fit your interests/skills
- are irritable or impatient with coworkers, customers, or clients (feel pressure from them)
- work with an office bully
- use food, drugs, or alcohol to feel better
- think your supervisor (or micromanager) constantly undermines your efforts

If your values differ from how your employer does business or handles employees' grievances, you might find this predicament eventually takes its toll on you. When your job environment is chaotic, you need constant energy to remain focused, which can lead to exhaustion. Lack of social support and work-life balance make people feel isolated at work and sometimes in their personal life. Unfortunately, these issues cause more stress.

For workers everywhere, the economy may feel like an emotional roller coaster. Company mergers, employee layoffs, and budget cuts are common in the workplace, and the result is increased fear, uncertainty, and higher levels of stress. Other causes of stress include the following:
- Low salaries
- Excessive workloads

- Few opportunities for growth or advancement
- Work that is neither engaging nor challenging
- Lack of social support
- Having little to no control over job-related decisions
- Conflicting demands or unclear performance expectations

Effects of Stress

If we are stressed, our attitude affects the quality of our interactions with others. The better you are at managing your own stress, the better you become personally and professionally. Managing stress effectively is very important.

There are varieties of strategies available to help reduce overall stress levels in the workplace: taking responsibility for improving your physical and emotional well-being and learning better communication skills to ease and improve your relationships with management and coworkers.

Managing and Coping with Workplace Stress

After 30 years in the working world, I have learned a thing or two about workplace stress and burnout – and the importance of managing stress so it doesn't take over my life. During my career, I have witnessed how unmanaged stress can hold people back from succeeding. Understanding how to manage, minimize, and deal with stress can help you feel more relaxed and react calmly to stressful situations when they arise. When handling emotionally charged situations, stay focused on the present by disregarding old hurts and resentments, connect with your emotions, and hear both the words and the nonverbal cues being used. Resolving conflict in healthy, constructive ways can strengthen trust between people and relieve workplace stress and tension. If you cannot resolve a conflict, end the argument, even if you still disagree. Remember, no workplace or co-worker is perfect – and no project, situation, or decision is perfect.

Stress Relief

The first step in successful stress relief is deciding to make stress management an ongoing goal and to monitor your stress level. Stress management is not an overnight cure, but you can learn to manage your stress level and increase your ability to cope with life's challenges.

Once you manage your stress, you might propel yourself to new levels of success. These several stress management strategies discussed can help you fulfill your career, business, and life ambitions, while living a happier life.

Chapter 7
Doctor's Orders

Bed Rest

Too much stress can cause insomnia, and when you do not get enough sleep, you are vulnerable to even more stress. Getting at least 7 to 8 hours of sleep each night is critical to your well-being because it protects and renews your body and mind. When well-rested, you will find it much easier to keep your emotional balance, a key factor in coping with job and workplace stress.

Relaxation Techniques

Relaxation techniques are an essential part of stress management. Which relaxation techniques you choose doesn't matter: What matters is that you select a technique that works for you, and you practice relaxation regularly.

If you are an overachiever, you may put relaxation low on your priority list, but do not shortchange yourself, as everyone needs to relax and recharge. Relaxation is invaluable for maintaining your health and well-being and repairing the toll that stress takes on your mind and body. Almost everyone can benefit from learning relaxation techniques, which can help to slow your breathing and to focus your attention on the here and now. Common relaxation techniques include:

- Meditation
- Tai Chi
- Yoga
- Massage
- Relaxation music

Recharging Your System

Nothing leads to an anxiety attack faster than working too many days in a row. After working long hours without a break, you will, most likely, become unproductive, as well as mentally and physically depleted. And when exhausted, you may have trouble solving tasks.

Working long hours for a long time without time off will lead to stress, burnout, and poor performance. Working too much without taking time off can cause you unhealthy reactions like stress, fatigue, and negativity, making you lose focus and depleting your emotional and physical resources – and has been associated with a higher risk of heart disease and hypertension. The human brain needs recharging, or else it will run out of energy.

> "A growing body of scientific evidence explains what many of us have learned from unpleasant experience: Push yourself through too many hours or days of work and your brain starts to push back."
> —Minda Zetlin, Business Technology Writer/Speaker, Co-Author of *The Geek Gap*, and former president of the American Society of Journalists and Authors

Do not get so caught up in the hustle and bustle of life that you forget to take care of your needs. Nurturing yourself is a necessity, not a luxury, so set aside rest, relaxation time, and recharging time – so you can feel rejuvenated. You need to give your brain and body some rest. Taking even just one day off can help you reset yourself mentally and make it easier to have a clear head once you are back at work. Also, try to implement one or more of these activities every day, even if you are feeling good:

- Go for a walk
- Spend time in nature
- Call a good friend: Talk to close friends and family who understand and can relate to what you're going through. Having one or two close friends at work is a great support system for you.
- Enjoy a cup of tea or coffee: I treat myself to a cup of my favorite tea or coffee in the morning before I start working. I sip on this drink throughout the day as I work, which motivates and helps put me in a happy mood.
- Do something special for yourself
- Play with your pet

- Write in your journal, or curl up with a good book
- Watch a comedy show on TV (humor is a great stress reliever)
- Light a scented candle
- Play the piano, or listen to relaxing music
- Take a long bath, get a massage, or spend a day at a spa
- Gaze at the stars, or take a walk in the park in the evening to separate your mind, body, and soul from the issues of daily life.

An Expedia survey found that 45 percent of Americans agreed that upon returning to work, they felt "rested, rejuvenated, and reconnected" to their personal life after vacation, and 35 percent said they returned from vacation feeling better about their job, as well as more productive. Americans' responses may not be surprising in a culture where long hours on the job often are valued, but that is not always good for the individual, the family, or the employer. After taking a vacation, people tend to perform much better upon returning to their job.

Leaving work *at* work is one of the most important recovery strategies and probably the hardest. If you obsess about work when you are away from your job, no recovery can take place. Detaching from work with diversions at night reduces fatigue and promotes positive results the next morning at work.

For example, it's Saturday evening, but instead of relaxing and being out with your family, you are sitting in front of your laptop or your home computer. You notice there are a few emails you have to send out before Monday morning. In addition, you have a couple of projects to complete before your next meeting. You are tired and frustrated to find yourself working on what is supposed to be a day of rest. However, you remind yourself it needs to be done, so you push through. If you're anything like me, this will sound all too familiar, but these behaviors are bad for your brain. You talk to yourself so that you can focus and work harder, which is counterproductive. Your brain deserves a rest.

Following a Plan

Do you need time in the Intensive Care Unit (ICU)? That is, do you need to take time off work, go on a relaxing vacation, take care of yourself, or let others take care of you? Here are some great ideas:

1. **Nurture yourself.** Begin by paying attention to your emotional, physical, and psychological well-being. Taking care of yourself makes you stronger and feel more relaxed.

2. **Make time for fun and relaxation.** When stress interferes with job performance or your personal life, affecting your health, you should take action.

3. **Take a vacation.** Americans are overwhelmed by stress because they are not taking the vacation time they have earned and deserve. Nearly three-quarters of workers say they are stressed at work, with one in four reporting they are either very or extremely stressed. No wonder! Many workers leave their paid time off unused, despite near universal recognition of the importance and benefits of time off, from reducing stress to improving productivity when they return to work.

   "Overwhelmed America" revealed that workers construct many of their own biggest barriers to taking time off. According to a "Project Time Off" survey (2014), while 96% of employees recognize the importance of using time off, 41% of Americans do not plan to use all of their vacation days. The top reasons workers say that they leave vacation times unused include fear of returning to a lot of work (40%) and the belief nobody else can do their job (35%). The effects of a tough economy still linger. One-third (33%) of employees say they cannot afford to use their time off, and nearly a quarter (22%) of workers say they do not want to be seen as replaceable. Roughly three out of ten (28%) employees do not use all their time off, because they believe being at work will show greater dedication to their company and their job.

   Taking good care of your mental health means giving yourself the proper time to relax and unwind. Clearing your mind is good not only for reducing all the stress you accumulate during everyday life but also useful for taking a step back and reassessing what you are doing and what direction you are taking. Working around the clock may seem productive, but its negative effects on your body and the state of mind are far greater than its benefits.

This is why taking adequate time away from your routine is crucial. And taking time off is not just about quantity but about *quality*. A few hours of solid time off can make a huge difference. I have taken time off that was not as relaxing as some relaxing weekends, which is why the activity you *do* during your time off is very important.

In "Seven Benefits of Taking a Vacation," Natasha Withers, a primary care physician at One Medical Group of New York, supports this idea: "Rest, relaxation, and stress reduction are very important for people's well-being and health. This can be accomplished through exercise and meditation, but vacation is an important part of this as well."

Withers says that there are seven ways that vacation can benefit you:

- improves your physical stamina / mental health
- makes you more productive
- prevents and cures burnout
- increases your mental power
- helps you gain new perspectives

Taking a vacation gives you the time off that you deserve, and according to studies, vacations increase physical and mental well-being, as well as productivity and focus. Taking a work-free vacation means not responding to emails or voice mails so you can increase the benefits of taking time off. I cannot stress enough the importance of taking a work-free vacation, a vacation without your checking your work email or still doing some work. I have to practice this for myself. Several months ago, my husband and I took a weeklong vacation. Although hard to do, I turned off my cell phone and refused to check emails so I could enjoy my vacation – and doing so felt great. Do yourself a favor, the next time you take time off, try not to use your phone or computer. Only then can you truly take full advantage of your time off.

Employees who take vacations perform better at work and have better performance reviews because, overall, they do more work at a higher level of quality. Taking a vacation also boosts your heart health. Vacations allow employees to:

- return to work with a strong focus and new perspective
- gain perspective on everyday life
- take a break from their usual routines
- develop themselves personally and socially
- promote shared experiences among family or friends
- Decrease the risk of depression
- Contribute positively to family bonding, communication, and solidarity (if a family vacation!)

4. **Eat well.** Research has proven that eating healthfully is linked to overall well-being and can help you get through a stressful workday, maintain your energy, stay focused, reduce or eliminate mood swings, and improve your mental and physical health. You will have a healthier lifestyle if you eat lots of fruits and vegetables regularly and reduce your intake of red meat. And if you drink alcohol, drink it in moderation. Although alcohol may temporarily reduce your stress and anxiety, too much alcohol can cause you anxiety as its effects wear off. Drinking to relieve job stress may also eventually lead to alcohol abuse and dependence, which can lead to other troubles.

5. **Get plenty of exercise.** Physical activities help you sleep much better. Walking outdoors, golfing, or participating in a sports activity can be relaxing and help you combat and reduce stress. Regular exercise is an effective way to lift your mood, increase energy, sharpen focus, and relax your mind and body. And you need regular exercise or activity that raises your heart rate and makes you sweat. For best results, try to get at least 30 minutes of activity daily to raise your heart rate and help you sweat regularly. Participate in aerobics class, running, walking, dancing, swimming, or playing tennis. Put exercise time on your schedule; if you cannot allot the entire 30 minutes or more at a time, break up the activity into two shorter segments, which may make it easier for you to keep your exercise schedule.

6. **Focus on what you can control.** Many situations at work, particularly the behavior of your supervisor and coworkers, are beyond our control. Rather than stressing out over them, focus on the things you *can* control, e.g., the way you *react* to the problems and issues. You cannot prevent or change stressors.

The best way to cope with stress is to accept things as they are, which may be difficult, but doing so is easier than going against a situation you cannot change.

7. **Stay positive.** Try not to complain when you have a different assignment. Times may be tough, but your negativity could make work more miserable for you and your coworkers. I know it is difficult to stay positive all the time, but positive employees make for a positive work environment. Reach out with positive energy to coworkers, even when you are running low on positive thoughts.

You can turn negative thinking into positive thinking. If you see the downside of every situation and interaction, you will find yourself drained of energy and motivation, so try to think positively about your work, stay away from negative people, and pat yourself on the back (if no one else does) about your accomplishments, even if they're small. Live in the moment, and maintain a positive mind-set.

All of these changes can increase your energy, improve your mood, and help you refocus your career.

Emotional Intelligence Spectrum

If you are in a job where the environment has grown increasingly stressful, you can still retain a large measure of self-control and self-confidence by understanding and practicing emotional intelligence, the ability to manage and use your emotions in positive, constructive ways. Emotional intelligence is about your ability to communicate with others in ways that draw people to you, overcome differences, repair wounded feelings, and diffuse tension and stress. It is important to have work satisfaction and success, but emotional intelligence matters just as much as intellectual ability. Emotional intelligence in the workplace has 4 major components:

- **Self-awareness:** The ability to recognize your emotions and their impact, while using gut feelings to guide your decisions
- **Self-management:** The ability to control your emotions and behavior and adapt to changing circumstances
- **Social awareness:** The ability to sense, understand, and react to others' emotions and feel comfortable socially

- **Relationship management:** The ability to inspire, influence, and connect to others, as well as manage conflict

When facing major challenges, try to look at them as opportunities for personal growth. If your choices contributed to a stressful situation, reflect on them and learn from your mistakes. Learn to forgive others. Accept that we live in an imperfect world and people make mistakes. Let go of anger and resentments. Free yourself from negative energy: Forgive others and move on.

Watching TV, lying on the couch, listening to relaxing music, reading a book, painting a picture, playing an instrument, or going on a trip are simple pleasures that seem to have become an impossible dream. However, forward-thinking companies, like Google, are known for their efforts to enhance creativity by giving employees time off to pursue ideas of their own, regardless of the outcome. Still, some of Google's most successful innovations have resulted from that policy.

Considering the price we pay in terms of our health and well-being, it may be time to question whether our traditional work ethic is still worthy or even sustainable concept. In their book *How Much Is Enough? Money and the Good Life*, authors Robert and Edward Skidelsky argue that people who work too hard miss out on the "good life" (although that is supposedly the ultimate goal of their intense efforts), but become rich enough to enjoy a happy, carefree existence.

The all-American creed that hard work will make us successful may still linger for a long time, but we need to accept our limits. Working harder does not guarantee success anymore, as taking time off and pacing ourselves isn't equivalent to laziness. Having a work/life balance requires making time for ourselves.

Remember that we are not robots: We are human, and we need to rest and heal. Although technology is nice and is supposed to enhance our lives, if we are constantly checking our emails on vacation, we're not away from work, bills, stress, and technology. Remember to disconnect and do something soothing and relaxing. You do not want to end up like the majority of Americans with high blood pressure (hypertension). Watch how being away from those distractions will positively affect your level of happiness and success in your career.

CHAPTER 8

Tami Gilbert
Good Behavior

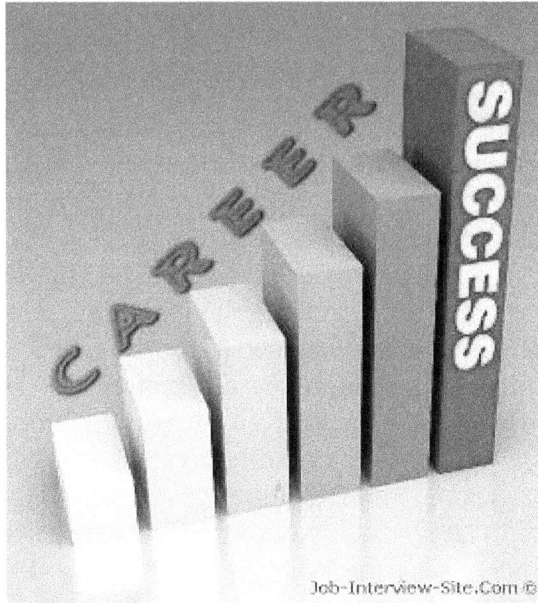

Job-Interview-Site.Com ©

Normal vs. Abnormal Behavior

Employees with a poor work ethic constantly complain about their jobs, colleagues, and the company. Some employees take long coffee or lunch breaks and spend a lot of time using the Internet, especially social media, for personal reasons. Such behaviors can negatively affect the work environment. Having a poor work ethic includes a lack of productivity, tardiness, and absenteeism, which can derail a career.

A good work ethic is defined as a value based on hard work and diligence. It coincides with morals that employees use to approach their jobs. Good work ethics include integrity, responsibility, quality, discipline, and teamwork: Essentially, employees with good work ethics go to work on time, do what they get paid for, and are reliable. Having a good work ethic is the key to having a successful career.

According to the article "Five Characteristics of a Good Work Ethic" by Erin Schreiner, individuals with a good work ethic are usually very productive people who work at a fast pace, regularly accomplishing more work and more quickly than those who lack a work ethic. Positive people do not quit until the work they are tasked with is completed. They desire to be stronger employees and to benefit their managers and the company, so if they arrive late, they will stay late to ensure the work is correctly done and on time. They also attend company events, such as holiday parties or picnics.

Two-Way Conversation

Add new responsibilities and engage more with your colleagues to bring value to your company and profession:

- Collaborate with your colleagues to help move you toward meeting department and company objectives.
- Ask questions and engage others at work so that you can find out how to add value to your career and company.
- Take initiative and request to become the lead for major tasks or projects. Your attitude can inspire others to follow you.
- Volunteer for different projects to help the company, even if you do not feel confident that you know enough in that area. Look at this as an opportunity to learn something new. Taking the initiative and leading others will help you stay connected to your colleagues, as you will be on the path of becoming engaged and productive.
- Continue investing in yourself by focusing on your career successes and achievements and by developing your skill sets and relationships. Thinking you have learned enough or believing you know enough people is counterproductive. You should learn as much as you can about your work, meet other employees, and learn about their work, maybe even making them aware of how you can help them.

Positive Thinking

Having a positive attitude and being helpful to others is vital. To maintain a great career, you must be polite and interact with your coworkers in a professional manner.

If you are negative, all you need is a strong commitment to improve your work ethic and 30 days of persistence and perseverance to kick your negativity. Not only will your supervisor appreciate your attitude, but your new approach will most likely provide you with a greater chance at advancing your career.

Stamina and Endurance

Remain ambitious by going above and beyond your regular duties and by exceeding job expectations. You can do this by looking for opportunities to work on new projects, expanding your skill set, and increasing your exposure throughout the company.

Risky Behavior

Today's job market requires that you be a risk-taker so that you can advance your career, so recognize risk as your new best friend. If you do not take risks and get involved in different projects, key stakeholders and decision makers will have difficulty understanding the value you provide to the company.

If you get involved with projects that contribute to your company's mission and vision, your visibility will increase. The decision makers will already know how effective you are and that you are a good asset to your organization. If the decision makers know your value, this will help to position you if the company reorganizes or changes in any way.

Bedside Manner

Understanding interpersonal relationships can change your life and career, and reading books on communication could help you become a persuasive communicator, a better problem-solver, and a more focused leader. For example, Stephen Covey's *The 7 Habits of Highly Effective People* can help you develop a take-charge attitude with confidence and enthusiasm. Also, Dale Carnegie's book *How to Win Friends & Influence People* provides great information for strengthening interpersonal relationships and ideas of how to manage stress, as well as how to handle fast-changing work environments.

In the article "Attitudes To Get You Ahead In The Workplace" by Yun Siang Long, the following characteristics can help you succeed in the workplace:

1. **Be enthusiastic about your job.** How can you feel enthusiastic about work if you feel *un*enthusiastic about it? For precisely this reason, I ask you to be enthusiastic. To be enthusiastic at work is a mental state, as you can choose to be enthusiastic. Long suggests you start by saying, "I will be an eager participant in this project or task." The more you tell yourself, "This is boring," the worse you will feel. Get interested in the work, and the energy will come naturally. Then decide to be eagerly involved. Being enthusiastic and energetic in the workplace is an attitude that can get you ahead. You cannot get ahead without

energy.

2. **Be efficient.** Strive to be the most efficient worker on your team. According to W*ebster's Universal College Dictionary*, being efficient means "performing or functioning effectively with the least waste of time and effort." When you are effective, you produce the intended result; when you are efficient, you do your work with the least waste of time and effort. That means you are capable and competent. If you constantly strive to be the most efficient worker, you will eventually get ahead in your career.

3. **Strive for excellence.** Of the five attitudes in the workplace, this one probably calls for you to put some pressure on yourself. A little pressure is good, since it makes you push yourself harder. Strive for excellence in everything you do. Do not be content with good: Go for *great*. Give everything you do your best. You will naturally see how striving for excellence in everything you do becomes your career booster, as you will naturally surpass others in your work.

4. **Show up on time or early.** Being on time or early will get you ahead in your career. If you start your day early, you can clear your emails and construct emails with a clear head and without being disturbed by other workers. When I start working early, I find that I am my most productive.

5. **Be easy to work with.** When you are easy to work with, you make working enjoyable for the rest of your coworkers. Such an attitude is welcome everywhere in the workplace, giving you a competitive edge (your career booster) on any team. If you constantly complain and are negative, others will find you difficult to be around.

6. **Be appreciative.** Most corporations today are looking for teamwork. When was the last time you verbally congratulated a coworker or threw a surprise birthday party for another employee? Create a more satisfying work life by looking for ways to celebrate your team.

7. **Volunteer your time.** Learn how to give your time, as your extra effort will show that you are a hard worker who is kind and interested in helping others and making a difference. Do not limit your efforts to office-related events: You can coordinate

with other coworkers to volunteer to help a local school or serve food at a homeless shelter. Doing good work outside the office with your coworkers helps you bond with each other.

8. **Have a positive attitude.** If you spend eight hours a day at work, why not make it more than just tolerable? Try to smile, laugh, and enjoy your job. If you work to create a more positive attitude in the workplace, others will follow. Having a positive attitude at work will reflect on what you do and make you a more productive employee. This can determine how well you do your projects and how others perceive you. If you display a good attitude and are a positive role model, you may increase your chances for a promotion or a raise. Employers want to promote people whose contributions add value to the organization. People who collaborate well with others can build on other people's ideas and encourage a higher level of innovation, as well as critical thinking, compared to simply pointing out faults in others' work.

9. **Become a better coworker.** When you walk into the office, smile and greet everyone with a cheery "Good morning!" If you do not do this, your coworkers might ignore or avoid you. Being cordial does not mean you must feel good, but greeting everyone cheerfully can make your day much better. This might also break the ice and reduce tension in your work environment.

10. **Get to know your coworkers.** Show interest in your coworkers to help make them feel comfortable around you. When the opportunity presents itself, ask your coworkers about their hobbies and interests, e.g., their favorite music, films, books, and hobbies.

    One day at work, my coworkers and I were waiting for a meeting to begin and were exchanging small talk; one of my coworkers talked about her children in a very caring, loving way. Suddenly, I realized that she was a real person; prior to that, I thought she was the coldest person I had ever met.

    When appropriate, talk about your life outside the office to show people you work with another side of you.

11. **Do not gossip at work.** You want no one talking about you behind your back, so you shouldn't talk about other people behind theirs. When a coworker approaches you with gossip, do

not engage in it. Change the subject, or get back to work. When the gossipers realize you are not engaged in the gossip, they will quickly move on. Avoiding workplace gossip will earn you the trust and respect of your coworkers. *Remember:* You need not contribute to negative workplace politics, so avoid instigating gossip.

12. **Promptly return phone calls and emails.** Doing so is good workplace etiquette and will win you friends at work. If you fail to return emails and phone messages, your silence may delay them or make their job harder. Not being prompt may send your coworkers the message that they are not important.

13. **Give others credit.** Always give credit to your coworkers when they deserve it. If you don't, you will alienate them, and they will not be there for you when you need them. Let others know when someone has done a great job on a project. Embrace the attitude that we all win together.

14. **Be creative.** We all have potential to be creative, and being creative at work and nurturing your creativity is important to career success. People with innovative ideas are highly valued in the marketplace, and to be one of them, you must think in fresh, unexpected ways.

15. **Nurture your leadership skills.** Whether you are aware of it or not, you are continually leading yourself and others. You do not need a large team reporting to you to be recognized as an effective leader. In one leadership study, qualities such as assertiveness, adaptability, intelligence, and conscientiousness were cited as the most important leadership skills. Research shows that transformational leaders who are positive and inspiring and who empower and develop followers are better leaders. They are valued by followers and have higher-performing teams. Therefore, strive to improve your leadership skills and get the most out of life and your career.

16. **Educate and improve yourself.** Great employees demonstrate effective leadership skills and continue to invest in themselves, either personally or professionally. Great employees become great leaders with the following attributes: integrity, commitment to the work, knowing and believing in themselves, communicating their enthusiasm, and developing

good working relationships with other people. Never stop growing and learning.

17. **Be effective at work.** Although many of us like to think we are 100 percent effective at work, most of us have strengths and weaknesses that influence our effectiveness. Effective workers get exciting projects, win important clients, and are respected by their colleagues and supervisors. Here are some ways to be effective at work:

- Be honest and approachable
- Be able to delegate
- Be a good communicator
- Have confidence, a positive attitude, and good intuition
- Be committed and creative
- Inspire other people

More Normal Work Behaviors

Adopt a good attitude. People with a good attitude take the initiative whenever they can. According to a Mindtools.com article, they will help a colleague in need, pick up the slack when someone is sick, and make sure their work is done to the highest standards. A good attitude at work does more than just earn you respect and set standards for your work and your behavior: It means you take responsibility for yourself. This admirable trait is hard to find in many organizations. However, demonstrating ethical decision-making could open many doors for your career, so focus on adopting a good attitude at work.

Manage your time. Managing time effectively is crucial to success at work. We must be able to organize and prioritize our time and tasks. Having a to-do list will help you stay organized and focus on and complete the tasks at hand. Organized employees prioritize tasks and schedules, emphasizing important areas. They plan each task, breaking each task down into manageable steps, identifying what is needed to get started, while avoiding distractions that could cause them to deliver their tasks late.

To be a value-add to your organization and to advance in your career, being productive is important, so give 100 percent of yourself at work. There is always someone watching you, and that person might be in the position to recommend you for another position or promotion.

Set goals. We must know where we want to go and what we want to achieve in our career. We must set a goal and commit to it. Our goals must be specific, measurable, attainable, relevant, and time-bound. We have to remember to set goals that keep us motivated. The most important step in achieving our goals is writing them down to make them feel tangible. Then we must plan the steps to realize them.

Increase your visibility. Always look for ways to improve your profile at work and your visibility. Again, to get a promotion or another job, it might not so much be *what* you know but *whom* you know. Usually, the successful applicant is popular within his or her industry and company but must learn to build and maintain strong connections with influential people and colleagues. Make sure you represent your department and company well in company-wide gatherings. It is no secret that people who get noticed get the best assignments, while those who keep their heads down miss out on opportunities despite their hard work.

You can increase your visibility at work without bragging or stealing the spotlight from your colleagues. "Why be more visible?" you might ask. I have met workers who said, "I just want to come to work, do my job, and go home." Today, being good at your job is not enough, and it is not the only requisite for getting ahead in your career. If key people are not aware of you, you will likely miss opportunities to improve your skills, take on interesting assignments, and show off your skills and achievements. When the decision makers are not aware of you, they may pass you over for a well-deserved promotion, despite your hard work and good performance.

Never depend on your supervisor to help you increase your visibility. Unfortunately, some supervisor may feel threatened or intimidated by you, thinking you may take their job. I am not recommending you bypass your supervisor's authority: You must be careful, as you do not want your supervisor as an enemy. However, to be recommended for opportunities, you need to have a plan to maximize your exposure, which is especially important if you work remotely, as your coworkers might forget about you if they rarely see you in person. Many people feel uncomfortable at the thought of promoting themselves, so they assume a more passive role in the workplace.

Fortunately, there are many simple ways you can become more visible, even if you are not naturally outgoing:

Speak up in meetings, and learn to be an engaging speaker. Sometimes we feel uncomfortable sharing our ideas in meetings perhaps because we feel shy or worried about how others will react to our comments; however, meetings give us a great opportunity to demonstrate our knowledge and increase our visibility within our team or department. If you do not speak up, it is never too late: You can work on developing your self-confidence so you feel more comfortable being the center of attention. (Joining a local Toastmasters group helped me greatly in this area.) Also, learn how to be a more engaging speaker, so you can make an impact that is memorable for the right reasons; push yourself to say more when appropriate, even if this does not come naturally to you. Suggestions to help you speak up more in the meeting include reading the agenda beforehand and thinking about the questions you want to ask or the points you want to make. This preparation will give you the confidence to speak up.

Strengthen your relationship with your supervisor. For some people, building a relationship with their supervisor is easy; for others, it's difficult. Talk to your supervisor periodically about your work, even if there is a formal evaluation process. Use this meeting time to discuss what is going well, ask for suggestions on how to add more value to the department, and find out about opportunities to work on different projects and raise your profile.

Ask for high-visibility projects. When you ask for high-visibility projects, you must also be careful, because your coworkers or even your own supervisor may get jealous and feel threatened. The higher the impact the project will make, the more careful you must be. Look out for and ask if your team has a project that must be worked on with people in other teams or departments or if there are any assignments you could take on that have a big impact on your organization's bottom line.

Do not wait for your manager to assign these projects to you: Volunteer to work on them when you find out about them. They will help you build relationships with people in other parts of the organization, and you might get more exposure to decision makers, such as senior managers and executives. While you are doing this, make sure you are not making anybody else in your department look bad. *Never* step over other people to get ahead in your career: You may need some of these people in the end.

Be reliable. People like to work with reliable workers. If you are reliable, people can count on you and trust you will complete the project. You will earn respect and be held in high regard by your supervisor and coworkers. Being reliable has positive, long-term effects that can also advance your career. Make your goal to become a reliable worker whom others also view as a great employee.

Calm Down. Stress is the number one barrier to effective communication, as when stressed or overwhelmed, you are likely to misread other people's reactions and send confusing and mixed nonverbal messages. Take time to calm down before having or continuing a conversation with anyone. Effectively communicating reduces stress and promotes physical and emotional well-being, as both listener and speaker become calm when the listener is engaged.

Communicating Effectively

Handle constructive criticism. Part of nursing your career back to health is having the ability to handle constructive criticism. Not everyone is born to handle harsh criticism without taking it personally: Some struggle with receiving constructive feedback; others experience a racing heartbeat when receiving feedback on their work performance; certain people feel as if they are being attacked; others may become defensive. Such reactions are normal. Nonetheless, constructive criticism is valuable, as we eventually become better aware of areas we need to improve and become more successful in our careers and relationships.

The next time you receive constructive criticism, step back and think about why you feel defensive. If your first reaction is negative, stop and take a deep breath, and halt the negative emotions. Refocus on the content of the critique, and do not allow your emotions to take over. Remind yourself to remain calm and focus on how the criticism can improve your career. Remind yourself of the benefits of receiving feedback. Constructive criticism can help you to improve your skills, work production, and professional/personal relationships. Sometimes, receiving feedback from managers, coworkers, peers, or someone whom you do not admire is difficult, but always focus on the benefits.

When being critiqued, remain engaged, focus on what is being said, and do not interrupt the person critiquing you. Allowing the person an opportunity to provide feedback without interrupting them shows your respect and professionalism. Paraphrase what you heard, and ask for confirmation. This ensures you correctly received what was said. A sample response to show you acknowledge the feedback would be, "You're right: I did cut him off while he was talking, and I later apologized for that." A sample statement when seeking specific solutions would be, "I'd love to hear your ideas on how I might handle this differently in the future."

Also, ask questions to gain a better understanding of that person's perspective. Sample questions would be, "I was a little frustrated. Can you share when in the meeting you thought I overreacted?" or "Have you noticed me getting heated in other meetings?"

Always remember to thank the person for his or her time and for sharing the feedback – and you will need time to process the feedback. Expressing appreciation does not mean you agree with everything: It means you will consider the feedback. And a follow-up meeting is important, as you may have more questions, and it allows you an opportunity to confirm next steps.

Constructive criticism is an important step in identifying areas of improvement. Staying focused on the content of the feedback, asking clarification questions, and not taking the feedback personally will help your career to flourish.

Communicate Effectively. At work, we make phone calls, attend meetings, write emails, give presentations, talk to customers, etc., seemingly spending all day communicating with the people around us. If your goal is to work more effectively, being able to communicate well is essential.

Write Clearly. Be careful with workplace written communication, particularly email, as writing emotional emails and then sending them without first rationally thinking through your message is a bad idea.

Never send hateful or inciting emails. If you must send an email with serious content, write your message on paper first, and read it several times before you write it in email form. If you are not sure about the content, ask a trusted colleague or friend to read your email and provide feedback, which will help you decide whether or not you should send it. Far too many people have regretted sending emotionally charged emails a few seconds after hitting the "send" button.

How well you communicate in writing reflects on you, affecting people's perception of you and making a difference in whether you are considered for a promotion. If you write many emails every day, focus on only one topic in each email, as putting several important topics in one message will make it difficult for the recipient to prioritize and sort the information. If you need to bring up several points, number them sequentially or split them into separate messages with relevant subject headings.

Writing effective reports and presentations is important for communication. To become more effective in your job, learn how to write and communicate better. Your supervisor and colleagues will thank you.

Watch Body Language. The nonverbal signals we send out – eye contact, facial expressions, tone of voice, posture, gestures, and touch – are important, as nonverbal messages can produce a sense of interest, trust, and desire for connection *or* generate confusion, distrust, and stress.

People watch your facial expressions and your body language and will not trust what you're saying if your nonverbal communication contradicts your verbal communication. You might say, for example, how happy and excited you are about your new project, but your facial expressions might reflect anger.

Your body language should be open and relaxed for being open to what the other person is communicating to you. Even though you might disagree with or dislike what is being said, don't cross your arms, as you need to show you are open to the other person's ideas.

Also, show you are paying attention by maintaining eye contact with the other person. You don't have to agree or even like what is being said, but communicate effectively without making the other person defensive.

What you say is sometimes less important than *how* you say it. Effective listening requires that you not only listen but also pay attention to the speaker's body language and emotions. Therefore, you need to be able to accurately read and respond to the nonverbal cues that your coworkers give you.

Focus/Listen. Always give people your full attention and focus on what they are saying. You cannot communicate effectively when you are multitasking. Your inability to focus on the conversation also makes people feel disrespected, i.e., they're talking to you and you're working on your computer, checking your text messages, or watching the clock.

Also, when someone is trying to communicate with you, focus on what is being said instead of on what you should say next. If you are planning what you will say next, daydreaming, or thinking about something else, you will probably miss his or her nonverbal cues in the conversation.

As an engaged listener, you make the speaker feel understood, which helps you build a stronger, deeper connection.

Empathic listening involves listening with your ears, but more importantly, your eyes and heart. You listen for feeling, meaning, and behavior – and you listen with the right *and* left sides of your brain. You are dealing with the reality inside another person's head and heart.

Stephen Covey, author of *The 7 Habits of Highly Effective People*, said it perfectly:

> "Listen with the intent to understand. I mean seeking to understand. It is an entirely different paradigm. Empathic listening gets inside another person's frame of reference. You look out through it, you see the world the way they see the world, you understand their paradigm, and you understand how they feel."

Requiring more than the words you use, effective communication combines a set of skills, including nonverbal communication, engaged listening, managing stress in the moment, the ability to communicate assertively, and the capacity to recognize and understand your own emotions and those of the person with whom you are communicating.

More Communication Learning Options

- Enlist help from managers or leaders you admire and respect. Good mentors provide constructive feedback and professional coaching.
- Search for public speaking videos available on YouTube.
- Watch TED Talk videos, which offer excellent public speaking examples by internationally great communicators.
- Improve your public speaking skills and leadership opportunities by joining your local Toastmasters. Toastmasters provides employees with a great opportunity to learn to give presentations and improve their public speaking skills, as well as learn more about each other. In this low-pressure environment, employees acquire useful speaking skills they can use during client meetings and for giving presentations to company leadership. Some employers like Allstate

insurance company, Abbott, Estella, and AON sponsor Toastmasters clubs in their company. Check with your company to see if it sponsors Toastmasters, or find out how to start one in your company.

In today's highly informational and technological environment, it has become increasingly important to have good communication skills. Having a successful life, career, and relationships requires that you are skilled in communicating, the process by which we exchange information with others, attempting to convey our thoughts, intentions, and objectives clearly and accurately.

Ineffective communication might result in misunderstandings that could destroy your productivity at work and jeopardize workplace morale – while effective communication enables you to communicate even negative or difficult messages without creating conflict or destroying trust.

Effective communication, a two-way street, is not only how you convey a message so the other person receives and understands it the way you intended and you listen well to gain the full meaning of what's being said and make the other person feel heard and understood. Successful communication occurs when both sender and receiver understands the information the same way. Communication is about more than just exchanging information: It is about understanding the emotion and intentions behind the information. When people are speaking to you, give them your undivided attention, a sign of respect.

Considered the glue that helps you deepen your connection with others and improve teamwork, decision-making, and problem solving, effective communication is a learned skill, it is more effective when used spontaneously rather than as a strategy. A person who reads a speech rarely has the same impact as a person who spontaneously delivers a speech without using notes. Even though developing effective communication skills requires time and effort, the more effort and practice you put into it, the more instinctive and spontaneous your communication skills will become.

Great communicators make great leaders and can create a cooperative work environment. They are kind, respectful, supportive, self-confident, outgoing, and flexible – and they try to find solutions to problems. If you are a great communicator, people will want to work with you, which can help you advance your career.

Building effective communication skills benefits your career because effective communication validates your professionalism and business reputation. If you are an entrepreneur, this increases your chance of acquiring new customers or getting more business from current customers.

Workplace Politics and Strategies

Workplace politics exists in every organization and includes strategies people use to gain personal or professional advantage in the workplace. It often has a negative connotation and adversely affects the work environment. However, when used properly, workplace politics can help advance your career.

To deal with and use workplace politics in a positive way, you must first accept the reality that workplace politics is here to stay. Then develop strategies to deal with your organization's political behavior. To help you develop strategies, you need to make observations and ask yourself these questions about your organization:

- Who are the masterminds?
- Who really has the power and the influence?
- Who complains all the time, and who is quiet?
- Who has the respect of the majority?
- Who motivates and encourages others to succeed?

Once you know most people's roles in your organization, you will have a good idea of who does or doesn't have power and influence. Next, you need to understand the relationships among everybody:

- Who are the cliques?
- Who hangs out with whom?
- Who is friends with whom?
- Who has the most trouble getting along with others?
- Who are the gossipers?

There are spoken and unspoken rules in the workplace, with positive and negative sides – and there are cliques, so you might have to see how you fit in. For example, if you want to get a certain job, maybe you know somebody who has the power to hire you, so you are extra nice to that person.

Be aware of politics in the workplace, and realize there are risks when you share your opinions or ideas. Fear of upsetting the status quo or potentially disagreeing with your supervisor or colleagues might prevent you from speaking up. You do not have to agree with everyone all the time, but when you disagree, do it in a professional manner. If you do not take the risk to share or voice your opinions, people assume you have no opinion or that you are clueless about certain topics and your credibility will diminish. Being liked is not as important as being perceived as someone who contributes value.

Due to the negative reputation of workplace politics, many see workplace politics as something to avoid. However, to ensure career success, you must navigate the minefield of workplace politics. If you refuse to play workplace politics, you will miss what might advance your career or help your department achieve its goals. Some of your colleagues may have power and influence.

While smart politicking might help you get what you want in the work world, you should not compromise your relationships with your colleagues in the process. Remember karma: When you do bad things to others, eventually, bad things will happen to you. Learn to use your power wisely and positively while diffusing the efforts of those who abuse it.

To survive workplace politics and maintain a successful career, find ways to fit in by learning the lay of the land at work and how you can be engaged and fit in. As you observe people and the culture of your workplace, see who is successful and model yourself after them. Build relationships with your colleagues, your managers, and the administrators. Be friendly and courteous with everyone. Avoid taking sides, stay away from negative politics, and be careful about what you say to others, as you never know who is related to whom. Promote yourself by volunteering for projects, and represent your team positively. Use your workplace network to gain access to information you need to build your visibility.

Support System

The feeling of belonging to your work group is very important – have at least one person there on your side – and of sharing a common goal with your coworkers. Employees who work toward a common goal promote their interdependency to complete tasks that benefit the company or organizational group. A cohesive work environment increases employee satisfaction and serves as an incentive for employees to arrive prepared and willing to conquer the tasks of the day. Lack of cohesion within a working environment is certain to result in unnecessary stress and tension among coworkers. When employees do not get along, work suffers. Ultimately, cohesion in the workplace could be the success or demise of an organization.

Understanding the root of group formation, as seen through the progression of stages, is an important element in developing and maintaining cohesive relationships within the workplace. Prior to entering a group, team members usually differ in many aspects, including personal background, work ethic, attitude, and commitments. To best ensure cohesion and increase productivity for the group, team members must find common ground.

Renowned social scientist Bruce W. Tuckman identified and explained the critical factors, or stages, of building and developing groups. These stages explain the process of group unification and cohesiveness.

1. **Forming.** During this stage, group members learn about each other. Indicators of this stage might include:
   - unclear objectives
   - limited involvement
   - uncommitted members
   - confusion
   - low morale
   - hidden feelings
   - poor listening

2. **Storming.** As group members continue to work, they will engage each other in arguments about the structure of the group. Such arguments are often emotional and illustrate a struggle for status in the group. The storming phase includes:
   - lack of cohesion
   - subjectivity
   - hidden agendas
   - conflicts
   - confrontation
   - volatility

- resentment
- anger
- inconsistency
- failure

3. **Norming.** Group members establish implicit or explicit rules about how they will achieve their goal. They address the communication that will help with the task. Indicators include:
   - questioning performance
   - reviewing/clarifying objective
   - changing/confirming roles
   - opening risky issues
   - assertiveness
   - listening
   - testing new ground
   - identifying strengths and weaknesses

4. **Performing.** Groups reach a conclusion and implement the solution to their issue. Then group cohesiveness is developed. Indicators include:
   - creativity
   - initiative
   - flexibility
   - open relationships
   - pride
   - concern for people
   - learning
   - confidence
   - high morale
   - success

Among the most important factors in constructing group cohesion within a workplace is trust. Since individual employees possess their own values and beliefs, each team member might take time to develop trusting relationships with other coworkers. Once trust is established, employees can better focus on their individual tasks and trust that other employees abide by similar standards. Trust also permits employees who find themselves in an unfamiliar situation to share advice within their group. Ultimately, trust enhances connectedness among coworkers and promotes group cohesion.

Being part of a cohesive team is often important for employees to be happy at work and have a successful career. Team building promotes team cohesion and builds trust, productivity, and efficiency; team building exercises help establish stronger employee relationships, improving collaboration and communication.

Team Building

There are several ways for employees to build cohesive teams and improve morale in our workplace. Initiate or coordinate a team-building outing with your coworkers. Perhaps make these outings a family-friendly event so employees can bring their significant others and children. And plan activities for the children so adults have time to chat and get to know each other more personally. If work conflicts occur, hold the activity in a neutral location:

- **Field Trips.** Host or help organize a field trip once or twice a year, e.g., a trip to a local museum, sports event, or attraction.
- **Fun Activities.** Find fun activities you and your coworkers can engage in so everyone can interact with each other as friends rather than just as coworkers. For example, coordinate an evening for your team members to go to the movies after work.
- **Picnics.** Organize a company picnic (weather permitting).
  - o Plan a barbecue or picnic at the public park.
  - o Cater the event so no one has to cook or clean up.
- **Potluck.** All team members bring their favorite dish.
- **Volunteer Activities.** Volunteering gives employees an opportunity to give back to their communities as a group.
  - o Coordinate with a local nonprofit organization so your team can volunteer to help them.
  - o Plan a volunteer activity for your team at a local food pantry or pet shelter to improve morale and galvanize your team. Giving freely to others promotes a sense of gratitude and service.
- **Lunch-and-Learn Sessions.** Start a "Lunch-and-Learn" series, which allows employees to learn from and communicate with each other.
  - o Advertise these sessions by placing a sign-up sheet in the break room or sending out an announcement in an email or

newsletter or on the company's website.
o Invite employees to bring food for an office potluck.

As you and your coworkers participate in fun activities together, you will form bonds and develop deeper professional relationships. Make team-building exercises a company habit. Whether a monthly, quarterly, biannual, or annual team building activity, the quality of your time together is essential.

CHAPTER 9
Strong Medicine

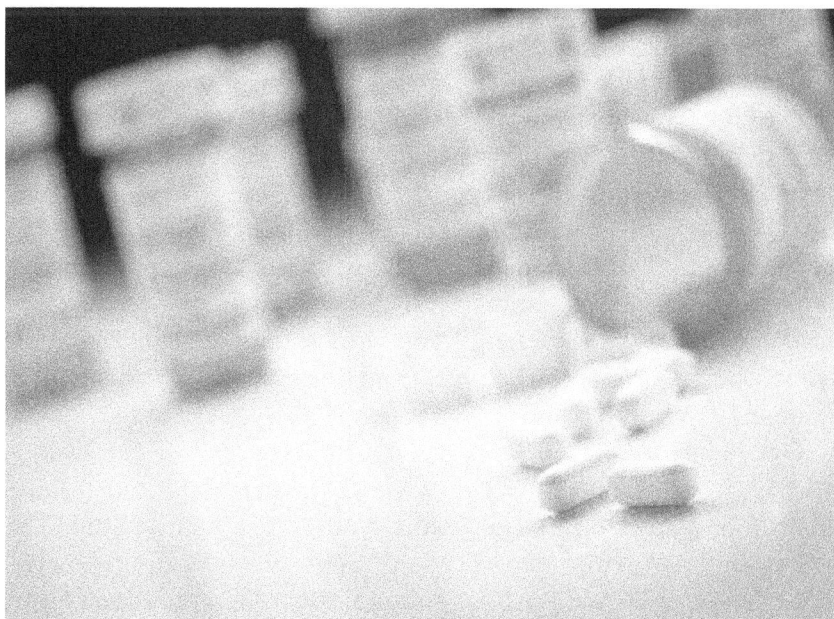

In this competitive job market, you need more than time on the job and the right degree to advance your career. The most valued employees in organizations often incorporate some strategies below to help them advance:

Apply your strengths, interests, and passion. Successful people, like Oprah Winfrey, state that an important condition for great achievement is passion. People who continue to advance their careers have high self-awareness, are in tune with their strengths and weaknesses, and live their passions. When you apply your strengths, interests, and passion to your work, you will feel powerful and strive to reach your goals.

Be eager to learn, and share your knowledge. As industries change and companies implement new ideas to remain competitive, they need employees who are eager to learn new skills, keep up with industry trends, share their newfound knowledge, and solve problems. People who enjoy learning new information and sharing ideas with others are invaluable to companies.

Be open to change. Change is inevitable, and companies deal with change daily. While employees who resist change are often the first to be let go, those who are flexible in times of uncertainty are embraced and valued. Companies need employees who embrace change and see it as an opportunity rather than as an obstacle. When you are open to change, your value increases, as you will be viewed as flexible. It is okay to become uncomfortable with change.

When possible, become a mentor. Job seekers looking for new or better opportunities like support and encouragement, and mentoring them provides them with this service. If you mentor someone, you have an opportunity to dramatically boost your confidence because by helping and teaching others, you remind yourself of everything you know. Also, mentoring helps you professionally, because others will see you as generous and helpful – and you can include this skill on your resume.

Get healthy and fit. Poor dietary choices, lack of exercise, and too little sleep are habits that can wear down the body and mind. If you want to be at the top of your game, you need to get healthy. That does not mean you have to go overboard. Start out exercising slowly, an act that alone will have a positive domino effect on your life. You will feel happier, sleep better, and get more work done.

Update your wardrobe to brand yourself. If you are serious about advancing your career, you need to take time to update your wardrobe. Have a suit or nice dress readily available, and update your hairstyle. I once heard someone say that you should dress for the next job you want because you never know who is watching.

Chapter 10
Long-Term Regimen

Your Healthy Goals

Make a 10-year plan. Creating a 10-year plan (shorter if it's easier for you) can help you more easily see what steps you need to take to achieve your goals. For instance, if you want a management position, plot out the path you need to take to get there. The steps might include talking to your supervisor, taking an accounting or business course, or volunteering for additional responsibilities. If you want to quit your job and start your own business, your 5- or 10-year plan might include saving money, obtaining financing, or finding a business partner. Dream big, target your destination, and map out how you intend to get there. Remember to *plan* to succeed.

Whether you have a 1- , 5- , 10- , or 20-year career development plan, a career plan will allow you to achieve your career objectives faster. Planning increases your focus toward your career goal. Once you develop a plan, regularly measure where you are in relation to your career goal. Whatever gets measured gets completed faster. Achieving your career objectives faster will likely contribute to the quality of your life. Planning helps you clear the unimportant and time-wasting activities from your life and gives you a sense of being in control again. As you write your plan, your career objectives, and the action steps you will need to take, you are forced to clarify thoughts and ideas about issues you would never have thought about otherwise. Thinking this way may open up different opportunities.

The following are a few simple tips on how to make and keep a 10-year plan:

- **Write down your goals.** Write down what you want, where you want to be, and what goals you want to achieve in the next 10 years.
- **Plan small steps.** If getting promoted at work is your goal, what can you do today to get started? Whether seeking a mentor or speaking with your supervisor, formulate an idea for immediate action.
- **What can you do this week, this month, next year?** Not all goals may be instantly achievable since achieving them sometimes first requires planning and preparation. Next year, get certified in a new skill, save up to start a business, or set a goal to begin a job hunt.
- **Embrace small wins.** Celebrate when you meet your milestones. A 10-year plan can give you the feeling that your goals are far off, so set your goals every six months or yearly, and reward yourself when you meet them.
- **Schedule regular assessments.** Evaluate your 10-year plan regularly to see what is and isn't working. You may need to adjust for contingencies along the way, such as a new job offer or a potential job loss. Allow no change in your workplace to throw you off-course. Do not give up. Look at any obstacle as an opportunity by recalculating your navigation and setting yourself on a new path to achieving your goals.

Taking Charge

Take responsibility for your career, as *you* are in charge of it. According to a recent survey, there is disagreement about whether career development should be the responsibility of an individual or an employer. In the September 2014 issue of *Forbes* magazine, Lisa Quest acknowledges that most workers believe the employer is responsible for teaching career development: "74% say employers should provide professional-development training, 71% say they should identify job opportunities and career paths, and 68% say they should provide career-advancement mentoring. Most managers believe employees must take responsibility for their career development: 98% say workers should continually update and improve their skills, 85% say they should identify job opportunities and career paths, and 80% say they should build their job-hunting and career-planning skills."

The results of this study demonstrate why many people fail at managing their own career. It seems like employers and employees often point the finger at each other regarding who takes responsibility for poor career development planning. Employer and employee should engage in honest conversations about what the end goal should be.

To increase the effectiveness of your self-advancement efforts, try to learn if your organization assists in creating specific career plans and timelines with milestones for achieving career goals. Find out about access to on-the-job learning opportunities – job rotations, job shadowing, mentoring, and targeted training – to improve certain skills and help you in your career development efforts.

If you work with a company that offers tuition assistance and career development programs, *you* are still personally responsible for your career goals, regardless of what your company offers. When there is a merger or layoffs, the companies usually do what they believe is best for the company, so you have to arm yourself with education, certifications, or continuing education units (CEUs). When you prepare yourself, you will not find yourself helpless, hopeless, angry, and depressed when layoffs occur.

While many companies have implemented career planning and training, not all employees are lucky enough to work at such organizations. This means you need to take ownership in driving your career advancement. The following are suggested strategies:

Define your career aspirations. If you do not know where you want to go, how will you get there? Define your aspirations. Where do you want to be in your career in 3, 5, 10, or 20 years?

Identify your goals, and create your career plan. Goals reflect what you want to accomplish to improve yourself and to move forward in your career. They help guide you in the right direction. They also help you achieve your aspirations quickly and efficiently.

If appropriate, share your plan with your manager. Ask him or her for feedback. Are there other skills you should learn, education you should pursue, or certifications you should obtain?

Find out about training and tuition assistance. Find out if your company sponsors training sessions you could attend. Maybe your company provides tuition reimbursement. Take advantage of every opportunity your company offers to help you advance in your career.

Remember: The person responsible for your career is *you*. Achieving career success requires more than luck and hard work: It requires a plan and forward thinking.

Career planning involves selecting the career suitable to your lifestyle, preference, family environment, and scope for self-development. Planning will help you prepare yourself for a promotion opportunity in your organization; it also increases your job satisfaction, enhances your commitment, and creates a sense of belonging and loyalty to your organization.

Career planning contributes toward your development, as a professional career development plan will help you achieve your career objectives. Of the many career strategies mentioned, this is probably the most valuable. Simply, career development is about setting and implementing goals related to your career.

Develop a professional action career plan with deadlines, reviewing it regularly to evaluate your progress, to keep your career in focus and on track. Take responsibility for your career's success and failure.

Emphasizing career development and training protects you from belonging to a stale work environment, where employees get comfortable in their current roles and do not reach their potential. Career development and goal setting keeps people on their toes, as they decrease their chance of being bored at their job since they have a goal to work toward.

One of the great benefits of implementing a professional career development plan is that the process usually forces you to identify your inborn job skills and earn money sooner. The people paid the most in any field are usually the people who are the best in their field, as they consciously use their innate, inborn abilities in their job. These skills are those they are naturally motivated to use.

There is no other way of more effectively increasing your income than by finding a job fit, where your natural inborn abilities match the work you are doing. Many people try to do this without getting this critical foundation in place, so they become frustrated with their job.

As the saying goes, people who do not plan to succeed might as well plan to fail. People do not plan to fail: They fail to plan. Evidence suggests that planning in *any* area of our life produces better results than not planning. Everything we do in life requires planning, including reaching our successful career destination.

Switching Plans

The prospect of changing careers is both exhilarating and daunting. If you know exactly what you want to pursue, do not become intimidated by the enormous challenges the career-change process presents. Employ powerful strategies to make that career change a reality. Conduct an inventory of your skills and experiences so you can leverage them in your career switch.

Company Type. Leverage your knowledge about the companies where you have worked. Nonprofit organizations have certain similarities, as do family-owned or owner-operated businesses and, to a certain degree, public companies.

Transferable Skills. Certain skills you have learned in one career will usually be relevant in the next. Project management, team leadership, sales, customer service, analytical capabilities, problem solving, hiring, training, and numerous others are all common transferable skills.

Experience. Use any start-up, shutdown, merger, product launch, or corporate crisis you have lived through as leverage when you talk to companies dealing with similar issues.

Job Environment. If you have ever worked in a high-pressure environment, you will recognize a similar environment in another industry. The same is true if you have ever dealt with unions or worked for an entrepreneur or without supervision.

Self-Confidence

When you combine your natural inborn skills with increased self-confidence, you push the boundaries a little more than you otherwise would. Doing so results in increased successful outcomes, e.g., an improved career. You will be recognized for your improved skills, knowledge, and expertise, which increases your self-confidence.

Evaluating Your Progress

To achieve your career goals, you must evaluate your progress and adapt accordingly. To achieve success, set goals often and continuously work on them. Below is a systematic process for creating a career development plan, which should include the following:

- Your career goal title
- The date you set the goal
- The target finish date
- Actual date the goal was achieved

As with any plan, your career development plan must be specific, measurable, attainable, realistic, and time-bound. In "How to Set Goals: 10 Steps to Stay Focused," Sarah Hanson developed a 5-step goal-setting plan describing each goal:

1. Specific. Your goal must be well-defined: Ask yourself the "what, where, and who" questions about your goal. Explain precisely what you want to accomplish, e.g., "My goal is to become a project manager in the medical field."

2. Measurable. For goals to be measurable, set a due date to help you know exactly when you reach your career development goals, e.g., "I want to be a project manager by January 1, 2020."

3. Attainable. Your goal must be attainable, achievable, and realistic. For example, if you want to become a project manager, what can you do between now and January 1, 2020, to achieve this goal? Are you working in the project management (or similar) field? What are you doing to acquire the skills/education to become a project manager?

4. Realistic: A goal must be attainable and realistic. For example, if I am a certified nurse assistant and my goal is to be VP of Nursing in a hospital in two years, my goal would be unrealistic if I were not in school or taking any classes. Therefore, implementing a plan helps guarantee that you will reach your goals. Your career goal must be relevant, regarding where you are right now and where you want to be with your long-term career goals. Is your goal relevant to who you are as a person and what you want to achieve in your life? Is this career goal in line with your passion?

5. Time-bound. Your career goals must have a timeline: a specific date you want to achieve this goal. Put the date from the beginning to the date you achieve it.

Chapter 11
Advocate for a Healthy Career

Your Destiny

Career success requires you to accept personal responsibility for your career, as you are in charge of your destiny. If something bad happens, step back, assess the situation, develop a plan to resolve it, and implement that plan. Making excuses or blaming others or external factors is counterproductive. Use such challenges as opportunities to grow and learn something new about yourself. You are empowered when you take responsibility for your actions, even if the situation seems difficult.

Endless Possibilities

Believe that almost anything is possible when you consider your career success path. Nearly every position and every project is within your reach. Do not just sit and talk about your dreams: Believe you can attain them, and set out to ask for what you want.

Life Experiences

If you learn from your mistakes, your experience is not wasted, as mistakes are setbacks (life experiences). Use these setbacks to help you become a better person. Your attitude toward challenges will determine how successful you become, both professionally and personally. Do not waste time lamenting your mistakes: Learn from them, and keep moving. Develop a positive attitude at work, and you will see your chances of succeeding increase.

Realizing Your Power

When you accept that everything you become is up to you, you avoid excuses that hinder your success. Avoid blaming others if your professional or personal life isn't going well. Instead, make a positive choice to view the circumstances as challenges and learning opportunities that can lead you to more success. Acknowledge your responsibility for your actions: You are not limited in what you can achieve.

Accepting Responsibility

Once you accept responsibility for everything that happens to you, you will soon discover you can find solutions to life's difficulties. If you are having a problem with a colleague or friend and the stress is overwhelming you, the stress will continue unless you empower yourself: Have a conversation with that person to solve the problem, and don't let the situation overpower you. When we are not happy with any situation and we take responsibility for it, we can find the solution. These are the key points to remember:

- When you are personally accountable, you take ownership of what happens because of your choices and actions.
- You do not blame others or make excuses.
- You do what you can to make amends when things go wrong.
- To become more accountable, you have to make sure you are clear about your roles and responsibilities.
- You are honest with yourself and others, admit when you are wrong, apologize, and move on.

Time Limits

You achieve success when you are honest with yourself and others. Set aside your pride, acknowledge your mistakes, tune into your instincts, and (if struggling) ask for help. Avoid making excuses; instead, focus on solving problems.

Knowing your limits helps you avoid unnecessary disappointments. Carefully consider time and resource requirements before agreeing to take on new tasks. If unsure, request more time to make a sound decision. These considerations will help you maintain strong relationships and a good reputation.

Chapter 12
Prescription for Success

Your Team

Surround yourself with supportive people who add value to your life, goals, and career. Create a team comprised of your family, friends, and colleagues in your field of interest. Including the right people on your team is crucial, so be strategic regarding whom you choose as part of your team, as you want people who are on your side and believe in you. Their contributions can be for emotional and/or professional support. Choose those who are subject-matter experts in specific areas in which you need guidance. You may need a financial advisor, fitness coach, teacher, or someone to talk to about personal matters.

Healthy Career-Life Plan

Have a Can-Do Attitude. To sustain a strong career heartbeat, you must have a can-do attitude and be positive in your ability to achieve career success. Your attitude controls every aspect of your life, influences the successful outcome of any task, and makes you the best choice for your next promotion.

Having an "I can do it" attitude as your life motto helps you take charge of your future. People with a can-do attitude are ready to take on anything: No challenge is insurmountable. They are positive, have answers for seemingly difficult problems (where they find opportunities), and do not get stressed easily. Cultivate a strong belief in your ability to cope with whatever life may bring.

Often, you can do nothing about your circumstances, e.g., losing a job or difficult situations at work. These situations can knock us off balance, but how we react to them determines how quickly we recover. Let go of the inner voice that criticizes you every time something does not go your way. Instead, analyze the situation and learn from it.

Develop self-confidence. People with a can-do attitude typically have a lot of confidence. Your being successful depends heavily in your believing that you can succeed and having a strong sense of self-worth, which means you know you matter. So, develop your self-confidence by building your self-esteem and being open to learning, growing, and paying special attention to yourself and those around you.

Develop the confident image you want to project. Select role models and learn from what they do. Improve your image and appearance. Make the most of yourself: Get a flattering haircut, manicure your nails, and maintain a healthy skin care regime. Take time to select flattering clothes and shoes. Dress to be professional *and* comfortable. Instead of focusing on things that are not working well in your life, focus on what *is* working well and on your strong points.

Concentrate on the positive aspects of your life. Look creatively at setbacks, and discover creative solutions. Stretch yourself, step outside your comfort zone, and boost your confidence even further. Review all the good things in your life, particularly your achievements. This approach will help you learn, grow, and move on. We always have a choice: to see the positive side of everything.

Learn to relax and have fun. View potentially stressful situations as challenges or opportunities. Above all, be enthusiastic about life and all that it brings. Remember, life is an adventure. Stay focused on your goals to keep motivated.

Being a Team Player

An effective team player communicates well and confidently. Great team players do the work, don't talk about others, communicate their ideas honestly and clearly, and respect the views and opinions of others on the team. Remember: You won't get ahead in your career by disrespecting other team members.

Effective team players go beyond what is expected. While getting the work done and doing their fair share is expected of good team players, great team players know that taking risks, stepping outside their comfort zones, and coming up with creative ideas is what it'll take for them to get ahead: Taking on more responsibilities and extra initiative sets them apart from others on the team.

An effective team player strives to do his or her best and does not passively sit on the sidelines but instead adapts to change. Effective team players strive to build positive work relationships and display genuine passion and commitment. They step outside of their comfort zone. Being an active participant and helping the team achieve its goals shows initiative, helping you to create a positive image, increase your visibility, and build influential professional connections.

Team Player Strategies

To achieve job satisfaction, take responsibility to make your job fun. The following are more strategies to help you bring more fun into your workplace. A great idea is to engage one of your coworkers to help you plan some of these fun activities:

1. **Make movie night a regular occurrence.** If you have a conference room or a place for seating and a TV, have "Night at the Movies" – and order pizza, snacks, and soft drinks. Make popcorn and enjoy classic movies or comedies.
2. **Have lunch outside or at the park if you have one close by.**
3. **Visit a museum.** If there is a museum close to your place of work, coordinate a trip to visit it with your colleagues.
4. **Have "Karaoke Night" at a local establishment.** Rent a karaoke machine, and follow the movie night theme. If you cannot sing well, then sing loudly and smile.
5. **Join a bowling league.** Attend a sporting event, or sign up as a team for a local 3K or 5K race. Whether you are a participant or a spectator, sports can be fun events to participate in together with your coworker.
6. **Have an office scavenger hunt.** Create teams of people to work together to find a list of items, either around the office or around town. A good scavenger hunt will last a few hours, yielding funny stories and solid bonding opportunities.
7. **Join a walking group outside of work, or form a group at work.** Joining a walking group gives you the opportunity to meet other people from different departments in your company.

This also helps you relate and get to know your coworkers, with whom you may have to participate on a project.

Celebrating Wins

When we accomplish a milestone, we should celebrate it. Sometimes, you are too busy to stop, notice, and celebrate what you have done, but don't lose sight of how powerful completing tasks is and how that success could mark the beginning of a new chapter in your life.

Make the most of such accomplishments so they have lasting impact. You are entitled to and deserve happiness and to be proud of your accomplishments. For example, spend the day with a smile. Share the joy with your friends and family. It is okay to let it be about you. Accomplishments, particularly those that involve happiness markers for those involved, are important.

Now that you have accomplished your goals, feel closure and contentment. Enjoy and think about them. Any realized goal deserves a respectful amount of reflection so you can grow and advance. Then look forward to your next goals.

Chapter 13
Positive Thinking

Benchmarks

An obstacle in your path becomes a benchmark toward success. Never forget that found in every obstacle is an opportunity to improve your condition.

Our approach to obstacles determines our ability to deal with them effectively. By controlling our irrational emotions, we can look at each of our obstacles objectively, see it as merely a temporary setback, and (if we continue to take action), reach our goals. The following are strategies for turning obstacles into opportunities.

Although failure is a lack of success, we are the ones who determine its impact. Maybe you did not satisfy a difficult customer, or you blew an easy sale at work. Maybe you did not do well on your presentation at work this week. Remember, failure is inevitable, but it does not have to define you.

Failure is the most important step in reaching success, but when it happens, it can feel like it is crushing our soul. To make failure our friend, not our enemy, we must overcome it.

We all make mistakes. The mistake does not matter: It is how we handle the mistake. It is a lesson learned and a stepping-stone to get you where you want to go. Mistakes provide us with the opportunity to change and improve ourselves.

When something happens that you initially perceive as negative, you need to look closely at the situation. You will find a positive, exposed benefit you can pursue.

"There is good in everything, if only we look for it."
—Laura Ingalls Wilder, Author, *Little House on the Prairie*

For example, if you have a bad supervisor, learn from his or her faults, while you update your resume and look elsewhere for a better job. If you face an obstacle, never stop taking action. *Keep moving.* Those who attack problems and life with initiative and energy usually win.

You always have an opportunity to flip a personal tragedy or crisis to your advantage. To do this, focus on something bigger than yourself. When you run into an obstacle and want to quit, think about those you are helping by doing your job and the effect of your work on them. *Remember:* Quitters never win, and winners never quit.

Therefore, when frustrated in pursuit of your own career goals, do not complain that you do not have the career you want. If you want opportunity, create it by getting started.

Persevering

Perseverance means being committed to hard work and staying focused. In my autobiography *Courage to Persevere: A Compelling Story of Struggle, Survival, and Triumph*, I share my story of how I persevered through life's difficulties, obstacles, and challenges. When I first arrived to America from Nigeria, I was living in a cold, dark basement because I couldn't afford a real apartment. I was a nurse assistant and wanted to be a Registered Nurse but didn't have money to pay for my tuition, so I worked two to three jobs to pay my tuition and make ends meet until I received my R.N. degree.

Choosing Happiness

"Most people are about as happy as they make up their minds to be."

—Abraham Lincoln, U.S. President

We must intentionally choose and take action to be happy. Happy people do not seek happiness in other people or possessions, and fully experiencing happiness each day requires a conscience decision on their part. So, how do we experience this joy? We can embrace new actions, practice them, or simply use them as inspiration to discover our happiness. Consider these strategies to help you choose to be happy today:

1. **Count your blessings.** Happy people thank God and focus on the positive rather than the negative aspects of life. Set your mind on specific reasons to be grateful, and express them when possible. There is always something for which to be grateful.

2. **Try to smile as often as you can.** If you smile at other people, you might brighten their day and yours, too! Research indicates that our facial expressions can influence our brain the same way our brains influence our facial reactions. You can program yourself to experience happiness by choosing to smile, and you will probably receive as many smiles in return, which may help to increase *your* level of happiness.

3. **Try to limit your complaining.** The next time you want to make a verbal complaint about someone at work, a situation, or yourself, think again and pause. Instead, keep your complaint to yourself. You will likely diffuse an unhealthy, unhappy environment at work. More so, you may experience joy by choosing peace in a difficult situation.

4. **Take care of your physical well-being.** Remember that your physical body impacts your spiritual and emotional well-being. Therefore, caring for your physical well-being can highly benefit your emotional status. One simple action to choose happiness today is to eat healthy foods. Your physical body will thank you, as will your emotional well-being.

5. **Treat others well.** Treat everyone you meet with kindness,

patience, and grace. Everyone seeks kindness, and deep down, we should treat others with the same respect we would like given to us.

6. **Meditate or do yoga.** Find time alone in solitude. As our world increases in speed and noise, the ability to withdraw appropriately becomes even more essential. Studies confirm the importance and life-giving benefits of meditation, so take time to make time. Use meditation to search inward, connect spiritually, and improve your happiness today.

7. **Always set realistic goals.** If you have no clear, concise vision of what you want in your career, business, or life, you can easily be led down a path that will cause you stress. Set clear goals in several areas of your life: family, health, career, finance, and spiritual, etc. By setting realistic goals in each area, you will create balance in your life, have a clear direction of what you want to accomplish in each area, and reduce your stress level, because you will have purpose.

8. **Master your attitude.** As I mentioned before, we can have a positive or negative attitude. The choice is ours. If you have a positive attitude, you will create more opportunities for yourself and feel refreshed. However, with a negative attitude, you will destroy opportunities and feel tired and stressed. During challenging times, negative attitudes become the norm, so choose to start your day on a positive note and carry that attitude throughout the day, checking yourself to ensure you are taking actions that guarantee a positive result. Also, protect your positive attitude when interacting with others. Use your goals and positive affirmations as motivators for success.

Managing Your Time

Focus on the Big Picture. During chaotic and challenging times, you'll be tempted to be pulled into activities and tasks that aren't important to the overall big picture. Then you will ask, "Where did the time go?" or "Why didn't I accomplish what I needed to do today?" These small or unimportant tasks might create stress. Prioritize each day so that you maximize your productivity and stay ahead of other employees in the same situation.

You can more effectively manage your time by incorporating some or all of the following strategies:

Manage your time, including external time wasters. Time management skills have a direct effect on efficiency, quality of work, and stress levels. Finding a time management strategy that works best for you depends on your personality, ability to self-motivate, and level of self-discipline. Take time management coaching with a personal development coach, read a time management book, or use time management software to keep you on track for achieving your success. Prioritize and organize your responsibilities.

Your time may be affected by external factors. You can decrease or eliminate time spent in these activities by implementing simple tips, such as minimizing frequent talks (unless work-related) with coworkers and avoiding small talk on the phone. If you have to make phone calls, stay focused on the reason for the call. Furthermore, always start and end meetings on time. And turn off your email alert messaging features on your computer so you will not be eager to check the emails that just came in, which can distract you from the task at hand.

Do you allow distractions to keep you from accomplishing more in your career? If you do, it becomes worse during challenging times. Take appropriate actions to manage your work style and stress. If you are easily distracted, make your work area distraction-proof. Turn off the email notification bell, turn your desk so it does not face the door, and control when and where you have conversations. By taking these simple steps, you can easily relieve your stress level at the office.

Poor time management can cause fatigue, moodiness, and illness (more frequently). Regardless of the time management strategies you use, take time to evaluate how they are working for you and to feel great about yourself and your accomplishments. Effective time management should lead to your having a healthy balance between work and home life. You also will accomplish the tasks that are most important in your life. Effective time management will reduce daily stress and help you be more productive.

Avoid multitasking. Routine multitasking may lead to difficulty in concentrating and maintaining focus when needed. Recent psychological studies have shown that multitasking does not save time. The opposite is often true: You lose time when switching from one task to another, resulting in a loss of productivity.

Set priorities. Managing your time requires that you make a distinction between what is important and what is urgent. One of the easiest ways to prioritize is to make a to-do list. Based on your lifestyle, you may need a daily, weekly, or monthly list. I recommend having only *one* to-do list, as more than one can confuse you and contribute to disorganization. To increase your productivity, use an electronic calendar, paper calendar, or computer program planner, where you can write your to-do list. Then send yourself alerts, so your mind is free to focus on your priorities. The key is to find one planning tool that works for you and to use that tool consistently.

Get organized. Getting organized keeps your mind clear so you can focus on the task and become more productive. Schedule your time appropriately (with high-priority activities for when you have the most energy), make commitments, and keep them. Also, know when you need help from others or have to delegate tasks to others. Delegating helps you free up some of your time for the tasks that you must be complete. You do not have to do everything by yourself. When you let go of the desire to control or oversee every little step of a task, you will let go of unnecessary stress.

Organize yourself for career success. Get rid of extra paper on your desk, because it is very distracting, as you might jump from pile to pile without accomplishing much. If you have piles of paper on your desk, organize and then remove them from your desk to place them out of your line of sight. Put these piles behind you if necessary so you can concentrate on the task and achieve more in less time.

Stop procrastinating. You may have many reasons for putting off completing tasks: Perhaps the task seems overwhelming or is unpleasant. If so, try breaking down the task into smaller segments that require less time commitment and result in specific, realistic deadlines. If you have trouble getting started, you may need to do prep work, such as collecting materials or organizing your notes. Also, try building a reward system for yourself as you complete each small task.

Live a healthy lifestyle. When confronted with challenges, some people tend to go for "comfort" food, as it makes us feel good but is generally not nutritious. Fried and sugar-laden foods, as well as dairy products, can increase stress levels and decrease productivity. Fruits, vegetables, baked chicken, boiled eggs, and plain yogurt with fruit are much healthier choices for lowering stress levels.

As part of your healthy lifestyle program, exercise 3 to 5 times a week. For example, take a walk around the office building or your community. Also, concentrate on stretching and breathing techniques that reduce stress, increase your thinking ability, and help you become more energetic and gain more energy to face challenging situations.

Get professional support. Counseling and personal development coaching are available to give you direction on your journey to a stress-free and improved working life. You will receive supportive listening and fresh insight, offload your worries and concerns, and share your burden of stress.

Being Proactive

Being proactive in your career is an ongoing task, helping you establish yourself as a serious and self-motivated person interested in moving up the corporate ladder. To be proactive with your career, you do not have to be aggressive and step over your coworkers to get ahead. Instead, you just need to continue to do the best job possible, volunteer for projects, be visible to the decision makers, wait for the opportunity to present itself, and be willing to go above and beyond in your job responsibilities. There are several ways to be more proactive in your career.

Be seen. Let colleagues/managers get to know you on a personal level. Attend corporate functions, even ones that aren't mandatory. Introduce yourself to those you do not know, and make it a point to say hello to higher-ups at every event. Learn to network and do more listening than talking, as being a good listener is invaluable. People love talking about themselves and their jobs, and you might learn some useful information about your industry.

Volunteer. Step up and volunteer to head committees, take the lead on a project, or be a project coordinator. Doing this shows your initiative and puts you into leadership positions. This approach not only makes you more visible to the decision-makers in your organization but also gives you valuable experience that will benefit you down the road. Join your industry associations, chambers of commerce, or Rotary clubs. Volunteer to speak at functions or to represent your company at industry events. This action lets your supervisors know you are a team player, giving you the opportunity to meet and network with influential people in your industry.

Participate. Always find something meaningful to contribute in a meeting, discussion group, or strategizing session. Be prepared for every group activity you participate in, so have something of value to share. Even if nothing comes to mind, acknowledge the validity of your colleagues' contributions. This will show your willingness to support your coworkers.

Set a career goal and achieve it. Participate in professional development and continuing education opportunities to move you closer to your objectives. Become a mentor. Ask for career guidance in setting short- and long-term goals.

Apply for promotions. If a position opens up that you are qualified for and are interested in, apply for it. Do not shy away from seeking more responsibility. Let your supervisor or supervisor know about the opportunities you want to pursue. If passed over for a new job, ask what you can do to better prepare yourself the next time such an opportunity arises.

Your success will create future opportunities. Successful people reap the rewards of their accomplishments by creating career opportunities. The process begins long before organizations seek someone for your ideal position. Successful people position themselves for success five to eight years in advance by identifying the right combination of experience they need to succeed in their ideal position. By instituting a career plan and working hard, you can prepare yourself for future opportunities.

Chapter 14
Characteristics of the Healthy Professional

People usually begin their careers, determined to meet their goals and make a positive impact in their industries. Many reach these goals. You probably wonder what sets highly successful people apart from everyone else. The article "Things Successful Careers Have In Common" by GovLoop (2015) suggests that the following are what sets apart those who reach their career goal from those who do not:

They stay organized. Successful career people have a system in place to track their career goals and achievements. There is no one-size-fits-all method for staying organized. Some people use journals, digital notepads, or lists. While these tools can help you set and achieve your career goals, whichever system you choose, staying organized will help you see the big picture of your career and plan more effectively.

They know themselves. Successful people know what they are good at, and they focus their energy on those strengths. (Profile tests like Myers-Briggs, DiSC, and Gallup's StrengthsFinder can help you understand yourself better by identifying skills you enjoy using, how you think, and how you work within a team.) They know where they are heading and have a plan, evaluating it frequently, even though they may not have an answer for every turn in their career. Therefore, think about where you want to go. Then map out the possible career paths to take so you can pinpoint the training you need or the people you should meet to make your next career move.

They keep learning. Always be where you can learn new things and develop new skills. Attending formal trainings, like professional conferences or talks by your specific industry leaders, are excellent opportunities for you to grow. However, informal education opportunities, such as career advice articles, self-paced online courses, and informal mentor relationships, are also great learning opportunities.

They track their accomplishments. They keep records of their accomplishments because career opportunities often come when you least expect them and frequently update their resume.

They invest in others to learn more about themselves and become better leaders. Becoming a mentor allows you to develop coaching/counseling skills and reflect on the value of your own experiences.

Conclusion

People with successful careers have clear plans with a concise structure put in place. If you want to succeed in life and in your career, develop consistent habits. Many of the greatest minds and most famous people in business and history got to where they did by developing habits and following very specific daily schedules.

Doing whatever it takes is the ultimate secret to career success. Life coaches, self-help books, and the Internet are readily available to most of us, so achieving career success should be easier for us.

Today's corporate America is evolving and constantly changing, so as workers, we must be prepared for uncertainty. Nowadays, companies do what they think is best for the company in case of mergers or layoffs.

As an employee, you must do what is best for you, so prepare yourself for the future by constantly updating and improving your skills, keeping up with industry changes, attending conferences, and regularly reading industry publications.

Take responsibility for your career success. If you do not do it, no one else will. You must take the initiative at work to make your job fun and interesting. Be proactive, take initiative, volunteer for projects, or accept with enthusiasm projects that help your company's bottom line. Doing this makes you visible to decision makers for the time you are ready for a promotion or another position.

When you do whatever it takes to get what you have set your heart on, you have no choice but to succeed. I have experienced this, it works, and it's very rewarding. Life really favors the willing worker.

When I was living in a dark, cold, unfinished basement, I never gave up: I knew I needed to get an education to improve my life and was willing to work two or three jobs to get my education so I could have a successful career and everything I wanted.

When we go all-out for our goals, something strange and wonderful happens. The very thing that seemed our greatest obstacle melts away. It is as if we were tested, but we passed with excellence. We feel as if we have learned what we needed to learn. Now we are fit to go on to the next part of our journey.

References

APA (2008). Stress in America: Press Room.
http://www.apa.org/news/press/releases/stress/

Arvind, Devalea (2013). "11 Tips to Develop a Can Do Attitude."
http.//www.arvinddevalia.com/blog/2007/01/16/11-tips-to-develop-a-can-do-attitude/

Belt, Hallie (2017). www.beltstyles.com

Blue Ninja 321 (2015). "The Willingness To Be Honest With Yourself."
http://answermug.com/profiles/blogs/the-willingness-to-be-honest-with-yourself

Braithwaite, Christian M. (2014). "Job Satisfaction vs Job Dissatisfaction."
https://www.linkedin.com/pulse/20140630173941-126410664-job-satisfaction-vs-job-dissatisfaction

Christie, Ian (2016). "Jump-Start Your Career Change."
https://www.monster.com/career-advice/article/jump-start-your-career-change

Clement, Sue (2016). "The Five Biggest Business Networking Mistakes and How To Avoid Them." http://www.businessknowhow.com/marketing/business-networking.htm

Collins, Teresa (2012). "Career Planning: 10 Strategies to Prepare for Future Success." https://www.besmith.com/thought-leadership/career-management/career-planning-10-strategies-prepare-future-success

Corso, Andria (2013). "Why You Need To Celebrate Your Accomplishments."
https://www.workitdaily.com/celebrate-accomplishments/

Counseling Directory United Kingdom (2009). "Stress Management Tips to Enhance Career Success." www.counselling-directory.org.uk/counselloradvice9828.html

Cussen, Mark P. (2016). "Keeping Up With Your Continuing Education."
http://www.investopedia.com/articles/professionaleducation/07/continuing-education.asp?ad=dirN&qo=investopediaSiteSearch&qsrc=0&o=40186

Davies, Simon (2010). "Six Ways a Career Development Plan Can Help You Achieve Fulfillment in Your Career." http://www.careers-advice-online.com/career-development-plan.html

Deese, James and Ellin K. Deese (1979). *How To Study*. 3rd ed. New York. McGraw-Hill Book Company.

Durham, Jeff (2016). "Taking Responsibility for Your Actions."
http://www.lifecoachexpert.co.uk/takingresponsibilityyouractions.html

Festinger, L., Schachter, S., and Back, K. (1950). *Social Pressures in Informal Groups*. New York. Harper and Row.

Folger, Jean (2016). The Complete Guide To Job Searching. www.investopedia.com/university/jobs/search.asp#ixzz4DUeDcAEe.

Galindo, Linda. (2014). "Choosing Accountability: 3 Steps to Owning Your Success at Work and in Life." http://career-intelligence.com/owning-your-success-at-work-and-life/

Garfinkle, Joel (2012). 5 Qualities That Makes a Good Team Player Great. http://careeradvancementblog.com/positive-relationships-team-members

Giordano, Louise (2016). "The Ultimate Guide to Job Interview Preparation." https://www.livecareer.com/quintessential/job-interview-preparation

GovLoop (2015). "6 Things Successful Career Developers Have In Common." https://www.govloop.com/community/blog/6-things-successful-career-developers-common/

Guest Author (2005). "How To Leave It All Behind You at the End of the Day." http://www.lifehack.org/articles/featured/how-to-leave-it-all-behind-you-at-the-end-of-the-day.html

Hansen, Sarah (2013). "How to Set Goals: 10 Steps to Stay Focused." http://www.lifehack.org/articles/productivity/how-set-goals-10-steps-stay-focused.html

Holiday, Ryan (2015). "10 Strategies for Turning Obstacles Into Opportunities." http://ryanholiday.net/10-strategies-for-turning-obstacles-into-opportunities/

Joseph, Jim (2014). "The People in Your Life Are Your Personal Brand Team." https://www.entrepreneur.com/article/230691

Lakein, Alan (1974). *How to Get Control of Your Time and Your Life*. New York. Signet.

Lindsay, Nicole (2012). "Taking Constructive Criticism Like a Champ." http://www.forbes.com/sites/dailymuse/2012/11/07/taking-constructive-criticism-like-a-champ/#4ede698958b7

Long, Yun Siang (2013). "5 Attitudes to Get You Ahead in the Workplace." https://www.workitdaily.com/attitudes-workplace-get-ahead/

McQuerrey, Lisa (2016). "Becoming Proactive in Your Career." http://work.chron.com/becoming-proactive-career-12838.html

Mindtools.com (2016). "Dealing with Office Politics: Navigating the Minefield." https://www.mindtools.com/pages/article/newCDV_85.htm

Mindtools.com (2016). "Developing Personal Accountability: Taking Responsibility to Get Ahead." https://www.mindtools.com/pages/article/developing-personal-accountability.htm

Mindtools.com (2016). "Overcoming Procrastination: Manage Your Time. Get It All Done." https://www.mindtools.com/pages/article/newHTE_99.htm

NYU Wagner. "Tracks Exercise."
http://wagner.nyu.edu/files/careers/TracksExercise.pdf

PaidTimeOff.com (2015). "Overwhelmed America: Why Don't We Use Our Paid Time Off?" http://www.projecttimeoff.com/research/overwhelmed-america

Papandrea, Dawn (2015). "Networking Tips to Advance Your Nursing Career."
http://nurse.org/articles/67/networking-tips-to-advance-nursing-career/

Pauk, Walter (1974). *How To Study in College* (2nd ed). Boston. Houghton Mifflin Co.

Pecoraro, David (2013). "Top 10 Ways to Clean Up Your Social Media Profile for A Job Hunt." http://studentcaring.com/top-10-ways-to-clean-up-your-social-media-profile-for-a-job-hunt/

Prive, Tanya (2012). "Top 10 Qualities That Make a Great Leader."
http://www.forbes.com/sites/tanyaprive/2012/12/19/top-10-qualities-that-make-a-great-leader/#2c8c38e03564

Project Time Off (2014). "Overwhelmed America: Why Don't We Use Our Paid Time Off?" http://www.projecttimeoff.com/research/overwhelmed-america

Quigley, Patricia (2011). "The Benefits of Taking Time Off."
http://www.usnews.com/science/articles/2011/08/17/the-benefits-of-taking-time-off

Raygor, Alton L. and Wark, David M. (1970). *Systems for Study*. New York. McGraw-Hill Book Company.

Reynolds, Jennifer Lea (2015). "10 Health Benefits of Taking a Vacation."
http://www.lovelivehealth.com/10-health-benefits-of-taking-a-vacation/

Speisman, Stephanie (Date Unknown). "10 Tips for Successful Business Networking." http://www.businessknowhow.com/tips/networking.htm

Staton, Thomas F. and Staton, Emma D. (1977). *How to Study*. 6th ed. Montgomery, AL.

Swart, Gary (2015). "Don't Stand Still: Take charge of your own professional development." https://www.linkedin.com/pulse/dont-stand-still-take-charge-your-own-professional-gary-swart

Tuckman, B.W. (1965). "Developmental Sequence in Small Groups." *Psychological*

Bulletin, 63, 384-399.

Whitmore, Jacqueline J. (2016). Business Etiquette Expert and Founder of the Protocol School of Palm Beach. http://www.aici.org/member/jacquelinewhitmore

About the Author

Tami Gilbert is a registered nurse, an author, and a motivational speaker who helps people achieve their goals by sharing specific steps and strategies to overcome obstacles, break out of a rut, and get on the path to prosperity, personally and professionally. She works in the healthcare industry and safety.

In search of a better life, Tami's father brought Tami to America from Nigeria. She always dreamed of becoming an American success story, so she earned her MSN and MBA degrees, because she realized that education was the way out of her struggle. Her life's mission is to inspire and motivate people so that they, too, can overcome anything that stands in their way of achieving their dreams in their life, career, and relationships.

Through years of struggle and persistence, Tami has achieved her dream of becoming a professional, a wife, and a mother. She is a member of The Illinois Organization of Nurse Leaders, American Case Management Association, and American College of Surgeons, National Surgical Quality Improvement Program, Illinois Surgical Quality Improvement Collaborative, Highland Park Chamber of Commerce, DBR Chamber of Commerce, and Chicagoland Medical Group Management Association.

Tami is available to conduct seminars, workshops, and keynote speeches for corporations, healthcare industries, colleges, nonprofit organizations, women's groups, and community groups.

Tami's speaking topics include:
- Increasing Employee Productivity and Maximizing Performance
- Strategies for Job Searches and Interview Preparation
- Work-Life Balance: Stress Management
- Turning Obstacles and Challenges into Opportunities

Coaching Services Available

Living a successful life and career does not come by accident. It comes only to those who invest time in learning exactly how to make it happen. The ***Achieve Your Dream Career Coaching Program*** includes an online course (*8 Powerful Steps to Achieve Your Goals*) and personal coaching.

This coaching program and the online course will help you learn how to choose your career goals, put action plans into place, track your progress toward your goals, and achieve your career dreams.

**For additional information,
contact Tami at info@tamigilbert.com**